About this book

Welcome to Kenya. The home of some of the fastest runners in the world. The home of UNEP headquarters. The home the Big Five animals. The home of giraffes that hug visitors and eat from their hands. The home of ostrich, tortoise and hot air ballon rides. The home of hundreds of national parks, game reserves, and animal sanctuaries.

This book, **Most Affordable Vacation Destination** is a must have for wild animal lovers who are looking for warm weathered vacations among very friendly citizens on a very pocket friendly budget. This book is a package of natural wonders, cultural heritage and tourism infrastructure that include but not limited to parks, ocean beaches, lakes, hot geysers, savannah, forests, snowcapped mountains, wildebeest annual migration and water sports.

This book is a menu of more than 50 of Kenya's national parks (one of it in the city), game reserves and animal sanctuaries. It gives you a "preview" of the tourism activities, landscape and climate.

Are you a conservationist? This book is awash with conservation efforts in place thus giving ideas on where you could plug in.

Accessibility to a destination in a foreign land gives visitors goose bumps. This book lets you into the national park, game reserve, and animal sanctuary of your choice by giving you direction and distance from your landing airport in Nairobi.

How about accommodation? This book lists lodges and hotels conveniently located within or nearest to the national park, game reserve, and animal sanctuary of your choice.

A gem for holidaymakers! Get your copy now!

Rose Muraguri

About the author

Dr. Rose Muraguri is a social scientist with doctoral qualifications in psychological counselling. She has close to 30 years combined experience as a high school teacher, university lecturer, a humanitarian worker and a counsellor. She does road trips for self-care. She loves animals and giraffe is her favourite. She is a diversity safe space counsellor and a mental health campaigner. Rose is registered and licensed by Ministry of Health (Counsellors and Psychologists Board). She is also a member of Kenya Counselling and Psychological Association (KCPA) and Kenyan Guidance, Counselling and Psychological Association (KGCPA).

Dedication

To you lover of nature and animals.

To you holiday-maker.

Introduction to a world-renowned tourist destination

Prelude

Kenya is situated in East Africa, bordered by Ethiopia to the north, Somalia to the east, Tanzania to the south, Uganda to the west, and South Sudan to the northwest. Kenya's capital city is Nairobi. The country enjoys political stability and a peaceful welcoming ambiance for visitors. Kenya has a vibrant and diverse destination renowned for its stunning landscapes, which range from the sweeping savannas of the Masai Mara to the lush highlands of Mount Kenya and the pristine beaches along the Indian Ocean. Kenya boasts an unparalleled array of wildlife, including iconic species like big five (lions, elephants, leopard, rhino, and buffalo), world famous wildebeest and pink flamingos, thriving in its numerous national parks, lakes and reserves. Kenya's rich cultural tapestry from over 40 ethnic groups and blended with Arab and Swahili influences that adds depth to its appeal, making it a top destination for both adventure and cultural exploration.

The country's diverse geography includes the Great Rift Valley, which runs from the north to the south, the fertile highlands around Mount Kenya, and arid lowlands in the northeast. Its coastline along the Indian Ocean features beautiful beaches and coral reefs, contributing to its varied climate and ecological zones. This strategic location places Kenya at a crossroads of African ecosystems, with savanna and tropical influences with a tincture of desert in Chalbi to the north shaping its landscape.

Geography and natural wonders

Kenya's geography is marked by its rich diversity, which contributes to its appeal as a tourist destination. The country features dramatic landscapes that include the Great Rift Valley, fertile highlands,

waterfalls and arid lowlands, as well as a beautiful coastline along the Indian Ocean.

Great rift valley: This geological marvel stretches from the Red Sea to Mozambique, creating a stunning visual divide in the landscape. The valley is home to numerous lakes and wildlife reserves, such as Lake Nakuru and Lake Bogoria, which are famous for their flocks of flamingos and other bird species.

Mount Kenya: The country's highest peak and the second-highest in Africa, after Kilimanjaro which is also accessible from Kenya, is a major attraction for trekkers and climbers. The mountain's glaciers and diverse ecosystems offer a range of outdoor activities, from hiking to wildlife viewing.

Coastal region: Kenya's coastline, with its white sandy beaches and clear blue waters, is perfect for relaxation and water sports. Popular beach destinations include Mombasa, Diani, and Malindi, which offer world-class resorts and opportunities for snorkeling, diving, and fishing.

Cultural heritage

Kenya's cultural landscape is as diverse as its natural environment. The country is home to over 40 warm hearted ethnic groups, each with its own traditions, languages, and customs. This cultural richness is reflected in the vibrant local festivals, crafts, music, and cuisine. The Maasai people, with their distinctive red dress, spears, clubs, red hair and high jump dancing, are one of Kenya's most well-known ethnic groups. Visitors often have the chance to experience Maasai culture through cultural tours, traditional dances, and visits to Maasai villages. Along the coast, the Swahili culture blends African, Arab, and Indian influences dating back to the Portuguese occupation which is evident in the region's architecture, cuisine, and festivals. Historic sites such as Lamu Island and Fort Jesus in Mombasa showcase this cultural fusion. The national museum located right in the city offers a melting pot of culture and the country's history for visitors to devour.

Tourism infrastructure and activities

Kenya boasts of near infinitive well-developed tourism infrastructure with a range of accommodations from luxury lodges and resorts to budget-friendly options. The country offers diverse activities, including guided safari tours provide opportunities for game viewing, birdwatching, water gliding and photography in some of the world's most iconic wildlife areas. Tourists enjoy mountain climbing, trekking, and hot-air balloon safaris cater to adventure seekers looking for unique experiences. Along the beaches, costal resorts and water sports opportunities offer relaxation and recreation.

Wildlife: national parks, game reserves and animal sanctuaries

The gist of this book is Kenya's renowned rich wildlife and numerous national parks and reserves that provide some of the best safari experiences in the world. This book explores 28 leading national parks, 14 of the biggest games reserves and 12 animal sanctuaries that are teaming with a huge variety of game some in the wild others in the confinements that make it easy see and take amazing pictures. Each of these wild animals abodes are discussed at length on location, Landscape and climate, wildlife, tourism activities, conversation efforts as well as Accessibility and accommodation opportunities. The book thus presents the reader with a wide selection of tourist destinations to choose from.

National parks covered

Aberdare National Park

Amboseli National Park

Arabuko Sokoke National Park

Central Island National Park

Chyulu Hills National Park

Hells Gate National Park

Kakamega Forest National Park

Kisite-Mpunguti Marine National Park

Kora National Park

Lake Nakuru National Park
Lake Bogoria National Reserve
Lake Elementaita National Park
Malindi Marine National Park
Marsabit National Park
Meru National Park
Mombasa Marine National Park
Mount Elgon National Park
Mount Kenya National Park
Mount Longonot National Park
Nairobi National Park
Ol Donyo Sabuk National Park
Ruma National Park
Saiwa Swamp National Park
Sibiloi National Park
South Island National Park
Tsavo East National Park
Tsavo West National Park
Watamu Marine National Park

Game reserves covered

Maasai Mara National Reserve
Samburu National Reserve
Buffalo Springs National Reserve
Shaba National Reserve
Boni National Reserve
Arawale National Reserve
Bisanadi National Reserve
Kora National Reserve
Mwingi National Reserve
Kakamega Forest National Reserve
Rahole National Reserve
Manda National Reserve

Dodori National Reserve
Ndere Island National Park

Animal sanctuaries covered

David Sheldrick Wildlife Trust (Elephant Orphanage)
Ol Pejeta Conservancy
Kisumu Impala Sanctuary
Sweetwaters Chimpanzee Sanctuary (within Ol Pejeta)
Giraffe Centre (A. F. E. W. Kenya)
Colobus Conservation (Diani)
Nairobi Animal Orphanage
Haller Park
Solio Game Reserve
Rolf's Place Animal Sanctuary
Ngulia Rhino Sanctuary (in Tsavo West)
Soysambu Conservancy

These national parks, game reserves, and sanctuaries represent a wide array of Kenya's diverse ecosystems, from savannahs and forests to marine environments, offering rich opportunities for wildlife viewing, conservation experiences animal adoption for the wildlife enthusiasts.

Kenyan national parks

Aberdare National Park

Introduction

Aberdare National Park, located in central Kenya, is a hidden gem among Kenya's diverse array of national parks. Established in 1950, the park covers an area of approximately 766 square kilometers (296 square miles) and is part of the Aberdare Mountain Range. Known for its lush, high-altitude forests, stunning waterfalls, and abundant wildlife, Aberdare National Park offers a unique experience distinct from the more open savannah landscapes commonly associated with Kenyan parks.

Landscape and climate

The Aberdare National Park is characterized by its rich, verdant landscapes, including deep valleys, dense bamboo forests, moorlands, and towering peaks. The park's altitude ranges from 2,100 meters (6,900 feet) to 4,001 meters (13,130 feet) at the summit of Ol Donyo Lesatima, the highest peak in the Aberdare Range. The park is also famous for its spectacular waterfalls, with the Karuru Falls plunging 273 meters (896 feet) in three steps, making it the tallest in Kenya. The cool, misty climate of the Aberdares creates a mystical atmosphere, with clouds often enveloping the mountains and forested valleys.

Wildlife

Aberdare National Park is home to a wide variety of wildlife, some of which are unique to this montane environment. The park is inhabited by large populations of elephants, buffaloes, and black rhinos, which are often seen moving through the forest and open glades. The park also hosts predators such as lions, leopards, and the elusive African golden cat, as well as a significant population of giant forest hogs, one of the largest and rarest pig species in Africa.

One of the park's most notable features is its population of the rare bongo antelope, a critically endangered species that thrives in the dense bamboo forests. Birdlife is abundant, with over 250 species recorded, including the Jackson's francolin, African goshawk, and the endangered Aberdare cisticola, a bird species endemic to the region.

Tourism activities

Aberdare National Park is less frequented by tourists compared to other parks in Kenya, which makes it an ideal destination for those seeking a more tranquil and intimate wildlife experience. The park offers a range of activities, including game drives, bird watching, hiking, and trout fishing in the rivers. One of the unique aspects of Aberdare National Park is its forest lodges, such as The Ark and Treetops, where visitors can stay overnight and observe wildlife at close quarters from the safety of elevated platforms. These lodges are famous for their floodlit waterholes, which attract animals throughout the night, offering guests a chance to see nocturnal wildlife.

Conservation efforts

Aberdare National Park plays a critical role in the conservation of Kenya's montane ecosystems and endangered species. The park's dense forests are vital water catchment areas that supply several of Kenya's major rivers, including the Tana and Athi Rivers. Conservation efforts in the park are focused on protecting its unique habitats, combating poaching, and supporting the surrounding communities through eco-friendly initiatives.

Accessibility and accommodation

The park is accessible from Nairobi, with a driving distance of about 100 kilometers (62 miles) to its eastern and western gates. The journey to the park offers picturesque views of the central highlands and is a perfect start to an Aberdare adventure. Accommodation options range from luxury lodges like The Ark and Treetops to public campsites for those seeking a more rugged experience.

Amboseli National Park

Introduction

Amboseli National Park is situated in southern Kenya, near the Tanzanian border, and covers approximately 392 square kilometers. Established as a national park in 1974, Amboseli is one of Kenya's most iconic wildlife destinations, renowned for its picturesque views of Mount Kilimanjaro and its large herds of elephants.

Landscape and climate

The park's landscape is characterized by its flat, open plains, which are ideal for wildlife viewing. Central to the park is a series of swamps and wetlands, fed by underground springs from Mount Kilimanjaro, which provide a vital water source in the otherwise arid environment. The backdrop of Mount Kilimanjaro, Africa's highest peak, offers dramatic and breathtaking views, particularly during the early morning and late afternoon when the mountain is often shrouded in clouds or lit by a golden sunset.

Wildlife

Amboseli is renowned for its impressive herds of elephants, which are some of the largest and most studied in Africa. The park supports a diverse range of wildlife, including lions, cheetahs, buffaloes, giraffes, and zebras. It is also a critical habitat for a variety of bird species, including raptors and waterfowl, which thrive in the park's wetland areas. The diverse habitats within Amboseli create a haven for these species, making it a premier destination for wildlife enthusiasts.

Tourism activities

Amboseli offers a variety of activities for visitors. Game drives are the primary way to explore the park, providing opportunities to see elephants, big cats, and other wildlife against the stunning backdrop of Kilimanjaro. Bird watching is particularly rewarding in the park's wetland areas. For a unique perspective, visitors can take hot air balloon safaris to view the landscape and wildlife from above. Cultural experiences are also available, with opportunities to visit Maasai villages and learn about their traditional way of life.

Conservation efforts

Conservation efforts in Amboseli are focused on protecting its unique ecosystems and wildlife, particularly its elephant population. The Amboseli Trust for Elephants, a key player in conservation, conducts research and monitoring to safeguard these animals and their habitat. Anti-poaching initiatives and community engagement are crucial aspects of the park's conservation strategy. The park's Conservation efforts aim to balance wildlife protection with sustainable tourism and support for local communities.

Accessibility and accommodation

Amboseli is accessible from Nairobi, approximately a 4-hour drive away. The park is well-connected by air, with scheduled flights from Nairobi to Amboseli's airstrip, making it a convenient destination for both domestic and international travelers. Accommodation options range from luxury lodges to budget campsites, catering to a variety of preferences and budgets.

Arabuko Sokoke National Park

Introduction

Arabuko Sokoke National Park, located on the Kenyan coast near Malindi and Watamu, is the largest remaining coastal forest in East Africa. Established as a national park in 1990, it covers approximately 420 square kilometers. This park is a crucial biodiversity hotspot, known for its rare and endemic species, making it an essential conservation area and a unique destination for eco-tourism.

Landscape and climate

The park's landscape is characterized by its dense, tropical forest, which includes a mix of coastal and montane forest types. It features three distinct forest types: mixed forest, Brachystegia woodland, and Cynometra forest. These diverse habitats create a complex and vibrant ecosystem. The climate is typically tropical and humid, with high temperatures and frequent rainfall throughout the year. The forest canopy provides a lush and cool environment, supporting a rich array of plant and animal life.

Wildlife

Arabuko Sokoke is renowned for its exceptional biodiversity. It is home to several rare and endangered species, including the critically endangered Sokoke Scops Owl, Clarke's Weaver, and the endemic Arabuko Sokoke bushy-tailed mongoose. The park also supports a variety of larger mammals such as elephants, buffaloes, and the rare Ader's duiker. Birdwatchers will find over 260 species of birds, making it a paradise for avian enthusiasts. The park's rich flora includes over 600 species of plants, contributing to its high ecological value.

Tourism activities

Arabuko Sokoke offers a range of activities for nature lovers and eco-tourists. Guided forest walks allow visitors to explore the diverse ecosystems and observe wildlife up close. Bird watching is a major attraction, with numerous opportunities to spot rare and endemic bird species. The park also features butterfly tours, which highlight its diverse and colorful insect life. Additionally, the proximity of the park to coastal attractions like Watamu Marine National Park allows for combined trips that include both terrestrial and marine environments.

Conservation efforts

Conservation in Arabuko Sokoke focuses on protecting its unique and endangered species, as well as its vital forest ecosystem. The park is managed by the Kenya Forest Service in collaboration with local communities and conservation organizations. Efforts include anti-poaching measures, habitat restoration, and community engagement programs aimed at promoting sustainable land use and conservation awareness. These initiatives are crucial in preserving the park's biodiversity and ensuring the long-term protection of its natural resources.

Accessibility and accommodation

Arabuko Sokoke National Park is accessible from the town of Malindi, which is approximately 15 kilometers away. The park is well-connected by road, making it easy for visitors to reach from the coastal cities of Mombasa or Nairobi. Accommodation options near the park include lodges and guesthouses in Malindi and Watamu, offering a range of amenities to suit different budgets. The nearby towns also provide additional services and opportunities for exploring the coastal region.

Central Island National Park

Introduction

Central Island National Park is a unique and remote park located in the middle of Lake Turkana in northern Kenya. Covering an area of approximately 5 square kilometers, the park was established in 1983. It is renowned for its volcanic features and critical role as a breeding ground for Nile crocodiles, making it an intriguing destination for wildlife enthusiasts and adventurers.

Landscape and climate

The landscape of Central Island is dominated by its three active volcanic craters, which have formed alkaline crater lakes filled with mineral-rich water. These craters, which are a result of volcanic activity, create a dramatic and otherworldly environment. The park's volcanic terrain is characterized by rugged lava flows, rocky outcrops, and sparse vegetation adapted to the harsh conditions. The climate is generally hot and arid, with temperatures often exceeding 30°C (86°F) and minimal rainfall, contributing to the island's stark, desert-like appearance.

Wildlife

Central Island National Park is a crucial habitat for Nile crocodiles, which use the island's warm, alkaline lakes as breeding grounds. The island hosts one of the largest crocodile populations in Africa, with thousands of individuals laying eggs on the sandy shores of the crater lakes. The park is also home to a variety of bird species, including flamingos, pelicans, and cormorants, which thrive in the alkaline waters of the lakes. Despite the harsh environment, the island's unique ecosystem supports a specialized set of species adapted to its extreme conditions.

Tourism activities

Tourism to Central Island is relatively adventurous due to its remote location. Activities primarily focus on exploring the volcanic landscape and observing the island's wildlife. Visitors can take boat trips around Lake Turkana to access the island and witness the crocodile population and birdlife. The island's volcanic features, such as the craters and lava flows, offer opportunities for geological exploration and photography. Due to the park's isolation, visits require careful planning and coordination, often involving permits and arrangements with local guides.

Conservation efforts

Conservation efforts in Central Island National Park are crucial due to its unique ecological features and the need to protect its wildlife populations. The park is managed by the Kenya Wildlife Service, which focuses on monitoring and conserving the Nile crocodile population and ensuring the protection of the island's delicate ecosystem. Efforts also include regulating tourism to minimize environmental impact and collaborating with local communities to support conservation initiatives. The park's remote location and specialized habitats require ongoing research and conservation strategies to address the challenges posed by climate change and human activities.

Chyulu Hills National Park

Introduction

Chyulu Hills National Park is located in southeastern Kenya, stretching between Tsavo West National Park and Amboseli National Park. Established in 1983, the park covers approximately 741 square kilometers. It is renowned for its stunning volcanic landscapes, lush green hills, and significant biodiversity, making it a captivating destination for nature lovers and adventure seekers.

Landscape and climate

The park features a series of volcanic hills and craters, which rise dramatically from the surrounding plains. The Chyulu Hills, which are relatively young in geological terms, are covered in a mix of grasslands, dense forests, and volcanic rock formations. The park's landscape includes notable features such as lava tubes and caves, including the famous Leviathan Cave, one of the longest lava tubes in the world. The climate is generally mild and temperate, with temperatures ranging from 15°C to 25°C (59°F to 77°F) and two distinct rainy seasons. The higher elevations of the hills receive more rainfall compared to the surrounding plains, contributing to the park's lush vegetation.

Wildlife

Chyulu Hills National Park is home to a diverse array of wildlife, supported by its varied habitats. The park's grasslands and forested areas provide refuge for animals such as elephants, buffaloes, giraffes, zebras, and antelopes. Predators like lions and leopards are also present, though less commonly sighted. The park's unique landscape supports various bird species, including raptors and forest-dwelling birds. The lush vegetation and volcanic features create a habitat that supports a rich variety of flora and fauna.

Tourism activities

Chyulu Hills National Park offers a range of activities that cater to different interests. Hiking is a popular activity, with trails that offer stunning views of the surrounding landscape and opportunities to explore the park's volcanic features. The park is also known for its horseback riding safaris, which provide a unique way to experience the terrain and wildlife. Caving enthusiasts can explore the extensive lava tubes and caves, such as the Leviathan Cave, known for its impressive size and geological formations. The park's scenery is ideal for photography and nature observation, making it a rewarding destination for outdoor enthusiasts.

Conservation efforts

Conservation in Chyulu Hills National Park focuses on preserving its unique volcanic landscape and protecting its diverse wildlife. The park is managed by the Kenya Wildlife Service, in collaboration with local communities and conservation organizations. Efforts include anti-poaching measures, habitat restoration, and initiatives to mitigate the impact of human activities. The park's role as a water catchment area is also crucial, with conservation strategies aimed at maintaining its ecological balance and ensuring sustainable use of its resources.

Accessibility and accommodation

Chyulu Hills National Park is accessible by road from Nairobi, which is approximately a 4-hour drive away. The park is also reachable from Amboseli and Tsavo, making it a convenient stop for travelers exploring multiple destinations. Accommodation options within and around the park include luxury lodges, tented camps, and budget facilities, catering to various preferences and budgets. Visitors can choose from lodges that offer stunning views of the hills and comfortable amenities, providing a base for exploring the park's natural beauty.

Hells Gate National Park

Introduction

Hells Gate National Park, located in the Rift Valley near Lake Naivasha, is one of Kenya's most captivating and accessible national parks. Established in 1984 and covering approximately 68.25 square kilometers, the park is known for its dramatic landscapes, including gorges, cliffs, and geothermal features. It is named after the narrow gorge that resembles a gate and provides a striking entry point into the park.

Landscape and climate

Hells Gate is characterized by its striking geological formations, including towering cliffs, deep gorges, and volcanic features. The park's most prominent landmarks include Fischer's Tower and Central Tower, which are remnants of ancient volcanic activity. The Ol Njorowa Gorge, a narrow ravine carved by water erosion, offers a dramatic landscape for exploration. The park's climate is typically warm and temperate, with temperatures ranging from 15°C to 30°C (59°F to 86°F). It experiences a bimodal rainfall pattern, with two main rainy seasons that support its diverse vegetation.

Wildlife

Despite its relatively small size, Hells Gate National Park supports a variety of wildlife adapted to its unique environment. The park is home to several species of large herbivores, including zebras, giraffes, buffaloes, and Thomson's gazelles. Predators such as lions, leopards, and cheetahs are present but less commonly sighted. Hells Gate is also known for its diverse birdlife, including raptors like the Verreaux's eagle and vultures. The park's geothermal activity provides a habitat for specialized flora and fauna, including various plant species and insects.

Tourism activities

Hells Gate National Park offers a range of activities that set it apart from many other parks in Kenya. One of the most popular activities is hiking, with trails that allow visitors to explore the park's gorges and volcanic features. The Ol Njorowa Gorge is a highlight, offering a scenic and adventurous walk. The park is also one of the few in Kenya where visitors can enjoy cycling safaris, allowing for close encounters with wildlife. Rock climbing is available on the park's cliffs, providing a challenging experience for climbers. Additionally, the park features geothermal springs and steam vents that visitors can explore. The Hell's Gate Geothermal Spa offers a unique opportunity to relax in naturally heated pools.

Conservation efforts

Conservation in Hells Gate National Park focuses on maintaining the balance between preserving its natural features and supporting sustainable tourism. The park is managed by the Kenya Wildlife Service, which works to protect its geological and ecological integrity. Conservation efforts include monitoring wildlife populations, controlling invasive species, and ensuring that geothermal energy production does not negatively impact the park's environment. Community engagement and education are also integral to conservation strategies, with local communities involved in protecting and managing the park's resources.

Accessibility and accommodation

Hells Gate National Park is easily accessible by road from Nairobi, located about a 2-hour drive away. The park is also reachable from other nearby destinations, such as Lake Naivasha, making it a convenient stop for travelers exploring the Rift Valley. Accommodation options around the park include budget lodges, campsites, and guesthouses in the nearby town of Naivasha. These facilities offer a range of amenities, catering to different preferences and budgets.

Kakamega Forest National Park

Introduction

Kakamega Forest National Park, located in western Kenya near the town of Kakamega, is the only remaining part of the vast equatorial rainforest that once covered much of East Africa. Established as a national park in 1993, it spans approximately 238 square kilometers. Known for its rich biodiversity and unique ecosystems, Kakamega Forest is a vital refuge for many rare and endemic species, offering an exceptional destination for nature enthusiasts and researchers.

Landscape and climate

The park's landscape is characterized by its lush, tropical rainforest, featuring dense tree cover and a complex undergrowth. The terrain is hilly and includes several small rivers and streams that contribute to the forest's vibrant ecosystem. The climate in Kakamega Forest is typically humid and temperate, with average temperatures ranging between 18°C and 25°C (64°F to 77°F). The area receives substantial rainfall throughout the year, with the heaviest rains occurring during the long and short rainy seasons, contributing to the forest's verdant appearance and high humidity levels.

Wildlife

Kakamega Forest is renowned for its impressive biodiversity. It is home to a variety of primates, including the rare and elusive black-and-white colobus monkey and the blue monkey. The forest also supports populations of forest elephants, bushbucks, and duikers. Birdwatchers will find over 300 bird species in the park, including the Great Blue Turaco and the African Pitta. Additionally, Kakamega Forest is rich in insect life, including various butterfly species. The forest's flora includes numerous plant species, many of which are unique to this forest type.

Tourism activities

Tourism in Kakamega Forest offers a range of activities designed to showcase its rich natural heritage. Guided forest walks are the primary way to explore the park, allowing visitors to observe its diverse wildlife and plant species up close. Bird watching is a major attraction, with opportunities to spot a wide variety of bird species in their natural habitat. The park also features trails for nature hikes and photography, providing scenic views and encounters with the forest's unique features.

For those interested in conservation, educational tours and talks on the forest's ecology and Conservation efforts are available.

Conservation efforts

Conservation in Kakamega Forest National Park focuses on preserving its unique rainforest ecosystem and the diverse species it supports. The park is managed by the Kenya Forest Service, which collaborates with local communities and conservation organizations to protect the forest from threats such as illegal logging and encroachment. Efforts include habitat restoration, anti-poaching measures, and community outreach programs aimed at promoting sustainable land use and conservation awareness. Ongoing research and monitoring are essential for understanding the forest's dynamics and ensuring its long-term preservation.

Accessibility and accommodation

Kakamega Forest National Park is accessible by road from Nairobi, which is approximately a 5-hour drive away. The park is also reachable from the nearby town of Kakamega, making it convenient for visitors from western Kenya. Accommodation options around the park include budget lodges and guesthouses in Kakamega and its surroundings. These facilities offer basic amenities and provide a comfortable base for exploring the forest. Some lodges also offer guided tours and additional services to enhance the visitor experience.

Kisite-Mpunguti Marine National Park

Introduction

Kisite-Mpunguti Marine National Park, located off the southern coast of Kenya near the town of Wasini, is a stunning marine protected area established in 1991. Covering an area of approximately 28 square kilometers, the park is renowned for its diverse marine life, pristine coral reefs,. and crystal-clear waters. It is a popular destination for marine enthusiasts and offers a range of activities that highlight the beauty and biodiversity of Kenya's coastal ecosystems.

Landscape and climate

The park's landscape is characterized by its extensive coral reefs, sandy beaches, and clear, shallow waters. The coral reefs are vibrant and teeming with marine life, providing essential habitat for numerous species. The park also includes several small islands, such as Kisite and Mpunguti, which serve as key ecological sites. The climate in the area is typically tropical, with temperatures ranging from 24°C to 32°C (75°F to 89°F). The region experiences two main rainy seasons, with a hot and humid climate during the dry periods, which are ideal for marine activities.

Wildlife

Kisite-Mpunguti Marine National Park is renowned for its rich marine biodiversity. The coral reefs support a variety of fish species, including colorful reef fish, parrotfish, and wrasses. The park is also home to several species of marine mammals, including dolphins and occasional sightings of whales. Sea turtles, including the endangered green turtle and hawksbill turtle, are frequent visitors to the park's waters. Additionally, the park's mangroves and seagrass beds provide critical habitat for a range of invertebrates and juvenile fish species.

Tourism activities

Tourism in Kisite-Mpunguti Marine National Park offers a range of activities designed to explore and appreciate its marine environment. Snorkeling and scuba diving are popular activities, providing visitors with the opportunity to experience the vibrant coral reefs and diverse marine life up close. Dolphin watching is another highlight, with the chance to see these playful creatures in their natural habitat. Glass-bottom boat tours are available for those who prefer to view the underwater world without getting wet. The park also offers opportunities for bird watching, especially on the islands, where various seabird species can be observed.

Conservation efforts

Conservation efforts in Kisite-Mpunguti Marine National Park are focused on protecting its delicate marine ecosystems and ensuring sustainable use of its resources. The park is managed by the Kenya Wildlife Service, which implements measures to prevent overfishing, coral damage, and pollution. Community engagement and education programs are integral to the park's conservation strategy, promoting sustainable tourism practices and raising awareness about marine conservation. Ongoing research and monitoring help inform conservation strategies and assess the health of the marine environment.

Accessibility and accommodation

Kisite-Mpunguti Marine National Park is accessible by boat from the nearby town of Wasini, which can be reached by road from Mombasa or other coastal towns. The boat ride to the park typically takes about 30 to 60 minutes. Accommodation options are available in Wasini and nearby areas, including lodges and guesthouses that cater to various preferences and budgets. Many of these lodges offer tour packages that include visits to the marine park, guided snorkeling or diving trips, and other activities.

Kora National Park

Introduction

Kora National Park, located in the northeastern region of Kenya, is a remote and ecologically diverse park that covers approximately 1,787 square kilometers. Established in 1989, the park is situated along the Tana River, which forms its northern boundary. Known for its rugged terrain, riverine landscapes, and rich wildlife, Kora National Park is a significant conservation area and offers a unique experience for adventurous travelers seeking to explore Kenya's more remote natural landscapes.

Landscape and climate

The park's landscape is characterized by a mix of savanna, riverine forest, and rugged terrain. The Tana River, with its numerous tributaries and seasonal floodplains, adds to the park's diverse geography, creating lush riparian zones and varied habitats. The park also features scattered hills and rocky outcrops. The climate is generally hot and semi-arid, with temperatures ranging between 20°C and 35°C (68°F to 95°F). The park experiences a bimodal rainfall pattern, with short and long rainy seasons that support the growth of vegetation and influence the river's flow.

Wildlife

Kora National Park is home to a variety of wildlife species adapted to its diverse habitats. The park supports populations of elephants, buffaloes, giraffes, and various antelope species such as impalas and Grant's gazelles. Predators including lions, leopards, and hyenas are also present in the park. The Tana River and its associated wetlands attract a range of bird species, including fish eagles, kingfishers, and herons. The park's riverine forests and savannas support a rich diversity of flora and fauna, making it an important area for conservation.

Tourism activities

Tourism in Kora National Park offers a range of activities that highlight its natural beauty and wildlife. Game drives are the primary way to explore the park, providing opportunities to see its diverse wildlife and varied landscapes. Bird watching is a popular activity, particularly along the Tana River, where visitors can observe a wide range of avian species. The park's rugged terrain and remote location also make it an appealing destination for adventurous travelers seeking a more off-the-beaten-path experience. However, infrastructure for tourism is relatively basic, and visitors should be prepared for a more rugged adventure.

Conservation efforts

Conservation in Kora National Park focuses on protecting its diverse ecosystems and addressing challenges such as poaching and habitat degradation. The park is managed by the Kenya Wildlife Service, which implements measures to safeguard its wildlife and natural resources. Conservation efforts include anti-poaching patrols, habitat restoration projects, and community outreach programs to promote sustainable practices. Given the park's remote location, conservation activities often involve collaboration with local communities and other stakeholders to ensure effective management and protection of the park's resources.

Accessibility and accommodation

Kora National Park is accessible by road from Nairobi, which is approximately a 6 to 7-hour drive away. The park's remote location requires careful planning, and visitors typically need to arrange for permits and transport in advance. Accommodation options within the park are limited and include basic campsites and lodges. Visitors may need to bring their own camping equipment if opting for a more rustic experience. Nearby towns such as Garissa offer additional accommodation options and services, providing a base for trips to the park.

Lake Nakuru National Park

Introduction

Lake Nakuru National Park, located in the Rift Valley of Kenya, is a renowned wildlife reserve established in 1961. Covering an area of approximately 188 square kilometers, the park is centered around Lake Nakuru, a shallow alkaline lake known for its spectacular birdlife and stunning scenery. The park is part of Kenya's Great Rift Valley ecosystem and is famous for its large flocks of flamingos, diverse wildlife, and varied habitats, making it a popular destination for nature lovers and wildlife enthusiasts.

Landscape and climate

The park's landscape is characterized by its picturesque setting around Lake Nakuru, which is surrounded by diverse terrains including grasslands, woodlands, and rocky escarpments. The lake's alkaline waters create a unique environment that supports a variety of bird species and influences the surrounding vegetation. The climate in Lake Nakuru National Park is typically temperate and semi-arid, with temperatures ranging between 15°C and 25°C (59°F to 77°F). The park experiences two main rainy seasons, which contribute to the seasonal fluctuations in the lake's water levels and support the park's diverse plant and animal life.

Wildlife

Lake Nakuru National Park is renowned for its birdlife, particularly its large populations of lesser and greater flamingos that often form impressive flocks around the lake. The park is also home to a variety of other bird species, including pelicans, herons, and ostriches. In addition to its avian residents, the park supports a diverse range of wildlife. Notable mammals include white and black rhinos, which are protected within the park, as well as giraffes, buffaloes, lions, and leopards. The park's varied habitats provide critical refuge for these species, making it an important area for wildlife conservation.

Tourism activities

Tourism in Lake Nakuru National Park offers a range of activities that highlight its natural beauty and wildlife. Game drives are a popular way to explore the park, providing opportunities to see its diverse animal species and stunning landscapes. Bird watching is a major attraction, with the park's large flocks of flamingos and other bird species drawing bird enthusiasts from around the world. The park's scenic viewpoints, such as the Baboon Cliff, offer breathtaking views of the lake and surrounding area. Additionally, visitors can enjoy guided nature walks and photography tours, which provide a closer look at the park's flora and fauna.

Conservation efforts

Conservation efforts in Lake Nakuru National Park are focused on protecting its unique ecosystems and wildlife. The park is managed by the Kenya Wildlife Service, which implements measures to safeguard its habitats and prevent poaching. Conservation activities include rhino monitoring programs, habitat restoration projects, and anti-poaching patrols. The park's role as a critical refuge for endangered species, such as the black rhino, underscores the importance of these efforts. Community outreach and education programs also play a key role in promoting sustainable practices and enhancing local support for conservation initiatives.

Accessibility and accommodation

Lake Nakuru National Park is easily accessible by road from Nairobi, which is approximately a 2.5-hour drive away. The park's proximity to the city makes it a convenient destination for both short and extended visits. Accommodation options within and around the park include lodges, campsites, and budget guesthouses, catering to a range of preferences and budgets. Some lodges offer luxurious amenities and guided safari tours, while budget options provide more basic facilities. Visitors can choose from a variety of accommodations that offer different levels of comfort and access to the park's attractions.

Lake Bogoria National Reserve

Introduction

Lake Bogoria National Reserve is situated in Kenya's Rift Valley, approximately 270 kilometers north of Nairobi. Established in 1973, the reserve covers about 107 square kilometers and is renowned for its geothermal activity, including hot springs and geysers, as well as its significant birdlife. The reserve's primary feature is Lake Bogoria, a shallow, alkaline lake known for its striking natural beauty and abundant wildlife.

Landscape and climate

Lake Bogoria National Reserve features a dramatic landscape dominated by the alkaline Lake Bogoria, which is flanked by rugged terrain and volcanic formations. The reserve is known for its geothermal features, including hot springs and geysers that create a visually stunning environment. The climate is typically hot and arid, with temperatures ranging from 20°C to 35°C (68°F to 95°F). The area experiences a bimodal rainfall pattern, with short and long rains supporting the reserve's flora and influencing the lake's water levels.

Wildlife

Lake Bogoria is famous for its large populations of lesser flamingos, which flock to the lake to feed on its high concentration of algae. The reserve is also home to other bird species such as greater flamingos, pelicans, and various raptors. Mammals present in the reserve include zebras, gazelles, and occasional sightings of larger predators such as lions and hyenas. The geothermal activity supports a range of unique plant species and invertebrates adapted to the hot, mineral-rich waters.

Tourism activities

Tourism in Lake Bogoria National Reserve offers a range of activities centered around its unique geothermal features and birdlife. Bird watching is a major attraction, particularly during the flamingo migration seasons when the lake's shores are teeming with these vibrant birds. Visitors can also explore the geothermal areas, where they can see bubbling hot springs and geysers. The reserve offers scenic drives and nature walks, allowing visitors to appreciate its diverse landscapes and wildlife. Photography is popular due to the striking natural features and wildlife opportunities.

Conservation efforts

Conservation efforts in Lake Bogoria National Reserve focus on preserving its unique geothermal features and protecting its bird populations. The reserve is managed by the Kenya Wildlife Service, which implements measures to prevent habitat degradation and manage human-wildlife conflicts. Efforts include monitoring bird populations, controlling invasive species, and promoting sustainable tourism practices. Community involvement and education programs are also essential in supporting conservation and raising awareness about the reserve's ecological significance.

Accessibility and accommodation

Lake Bogoria National Reserve is accessible by road from Nairobi, approximately a 4-hour drive away. The reserve is also reachable from nearby towns such as Marigat. Accommodation options within the reserve are limited, with basic campsites and lodges available. Visitors may also find additional lodging in nearby towns or along the route to the reserve, offering a range of amenities and services.

Lake Elementaita National Park

Introduction

Lake Elementaita National Park, located in Kenya's Rift Valley approximately 120 kilometers northwest of Nairobi, is a small but ecologically significant park. Established in 1989, the park covers about 35 square kilometers and is centered around Lake Elementaita, a shallow alkaline lake known for its birdlife and serene landscapes. The park is part of the greater Great Rift Valley system and is an important site for bird conservation.

Landscape and climate

The landscape of Lake Elementaita National Park is defined by the lake itself, surrounded by open grasslands and low hills. The lake's alkaline waters create a unique environment that supports a variety of bird species. The park's climate is typically warm and semi-arid, with temperatures ranging from 20°C to 30°C (68°F to 86°F). The area experiences seasonal rainfall, with short and long rains contributing to the park's vegetation and influencing the lake's water levels.

Wildlife

Lake Elementaita National Park is renowned for its birdlife, particularly its populations of lesser flamingos, which flock to the lake's shores to feed on its algae. The park also supports a variety of other bird species, including pelicans, herons, and various waterfowl. Mammals found in the park include giraffes, zebras, and antelopes, such as impalas and gazelles. The park's grasslands and lake provide important habitat for both resident and migratory species.

Tourism activities

Tourism in Lake Elementaita National Park is centered around its birdlife and scenic landscapes. Bird watching is a key activity, with opportunities to observe large flocks of flamingos and other avian species. The park offers guided game drives and nature walks, allowing visitors to explore its diverse habitats and spot wildlife. Photography is popular due to the picturesque views of the lake and its surrounding landscapes. The park also has designated viewing points for taking in the lake's natural beauty.

Conservation efforts

Conservation efforts in Lake Elementaita National Park focus on protecting its bird populations and preserving the lake's ecological balance. The park is managed by the Kenya Wildlife Service, which works to safeguard the lake from pollution and habitat degradation. Conservation activities include monitoring bird populations, preventing poaching, and managing human-wildlife interactions. Community involvement and education programs are essential in promoting sustainable practices and enhancing local support for conservation.

Accessibility and accommodation

Lake Elementaita National Park is accessible by road from Nairobi, approximately a 2-hour drive away. The park is also reachable from nearby towns such as Naivasha. Accommodation options within and around the park include lodges and campsites that offer varying levels of comfort and amenities. Some lodges provide guided tours and additional services to enhance the visitor experience.

Malindi Marine National Park

Introduction

Malindi Marine National Park, located along Kenya's coastline near the town of Malindi, was established in 1968. Covering approximately 213 square kilometers, it includes both marine and terrestrial areas. The park is renowned for its vibrant coral reefs, clear waters, and diverse marine life. It is a premier destination for marine enthusiasts and offers a range of activities centered around its beautiful coastal environment.

Landscape and climate

The park's landscape features an extensive coral reef system, with numerous coral species and marine habitats. The shallow, clear waters are ideal for snorkeling and diving. The coastline includes sandy beaches and mangrove forests, which provide additional ecological diversity. The climate in Malindi Marine National Park is tropical, with temperatures ranging from 24°C to 32°C (75°F to 89°F). The region experiences two main rainy seasons, which support the park's lush vegetation and influence the marine environment.

Wildlife

Malindi Marine National Park boasts a rich array of marine life, including over 100 species of coral and a variety of tropical fish, such as parrotfish, clownfish, and surgeonfish. The park is also home to sea turtles, including the green turtle and hawksbill turtle, which nest on the nearby beaches. Dolphins are frequently spotted in the park's waters, and occasional sightings of whales and manta rays add to the park's appeal. The mangroves and seagrass beds support a range of invertebrates and juvenile fish.

Tourism activities

Tourism in Malindi Marine National Park revolves around its marine and coastal environments. Popular activities include snorkeling and scuba diving, which provide visitors with the opportunity to explore the vibrant coral reefs and observe diverse marine species. Glass-bottom boat tours offer a way to view the underwater world without getting wet. Dolphin watching and guided boat trips are also popular. The park's beaches and mangroves are ideal for relaxation and nature walks.

Conservation efforts

Conservation in Malindi Marine National Park focuses on protecting its coral reefs and marine life from threats such as pollution, overfishing, and coral bleaching. The park is managed by the Kenya Wildlife Service in collaboration with local communities and conservation organizations. Efforts include coral reef restoration projects, marine patrols to prevent illegal fishing, and education programs to promote sustainable tourism practices. Research and monitoring are crucial for understanding and mitigating environmental impacts.

Accessibility and accommodation

Malindi Marine National Park is easily accessible from the town of Malindi, which is approximately a 2.5-hour drive from Mombasa. The park can be reached by boat from Malindi and Watamu. Accommodation options in Malindi and Watamu include a range of lodges, resorts, and guesthouses, offering varying levels of comfort and amenities. Many lodges provide packages that include guided tours and marine activities.

Marsabit National Park

Introduction

Marsabit National Park, established in 1948, is a prominent conservation area located in northern Kenya. Spanning approximately 1,500 square kilometers, the park is noted for its distinctive volcanic landscape and diverse ecosystems. Situated near the town of Marsabit, the park serves as a critical refuge for wildlife in one of Kenya's more remote regions. It is renowned for its unique combination of arid and forested environments, offering a rare ecological juxtaposition.

Landscape and climate

The landscape of Marsabit National Park is characterized by its rugged volcanic terrain, including the prominent Marsabit Mountain, which rises dramatically from the surrounding arid plains. The mountain's slopes are covered in lush montane forest, contrasting sharply with the surrounding semi-arid landscape. The park features a range of environments, from rocky outcrops and volcanic craters to grassy plains and forested areas. The climate is generally hot and semi-arid, with temperatures ranging between 20°C and 35°C (68°F to 95°F). The park receives more rainfall compared to the surrounding region, with a bimodal pattern of rainfall that supports its varied vegetation.

Wildlife

Marsabit National Park is home to a rich array of wildlife adapted to its diverse habitats. The park supports populations of elephants, buffaloes, and giraffes, as well as several antelope species, including Grant's gazelles and impalas. Predators such as lions, leopards, and hyenas are also present. The forested regions of Marsabit Mountain are known for their avian diversity, including rare species like Hartlaub's turaco. The park's varied ecosystems provide essential habitats for both resident and migratory species, making it an important site for conservation.

Tourism activities

Tourism in Marsabit National Park is centered around its unique landscapes and wildlife. Game drives offer visitors the opportunity to explore the park's diverse environments and observe its wildlife. Bird watching is particularly rewarding in the forested areas, where visitors can spot a variety of rare and endemic bird species. The park's volcanic features and scenic viewpoints, such as the crater lakes and the summit of Marsabit Mountain, provide stunning panoramas and opportunities for photography. The remote and rugged terrain makes Marsabit an ideal destination for adventurous travelers seeking a less conventional safari experience.

Conservation efforts

Conservation efforts in Marsabit National Park are focused on preserving its unique ecosystems and addressing threats such as poaching and habitat degradation. The park is managed by the Kenya Wildlife Service, which implements measures to protect its wildlife and natural resources. Conservation activities include anti-poaching patrols, habitat restoration projects, and community engagement programs to promote sustainable practices. Research and monitoring play a crucial role in understanding the park's ecological dynamics and guiding conservation strategies.

Accessibility and accommodation

Marsabit National Park is accessible by road from Nairobi, which is approximately a 10-hour drive away. The park can also be reached by flights to Marsabit Airport, followed by a short drive to the park. Accommodation options within the park are limited and typically include basic lodges and campsites. Nearby towns such as Marsabit offer additional lodging options, with varying levels of comfort and amenities. Visitors should plan their trip carefully and make arrangements in advance to ensure a smooth and enjoyable experience in this remote and unique park.

Meru National Park

Introduction

Meru National Park, established in 1966, is a diverse and scenic wildlife sanctuary located in northeastern Kenya. Covering approximately 870 square kilometers, the park is known for its rich biodiversity, lush vegetation, and varied landscapes. It lies near the town of Meru and is part of the larger Meru Conservation Area. The park is renowned for its role in the conservation of endangered species and its vibrant ecosystems, offering a unique and enriching safari experience.

Landscape and climate

The park features a diverse landscape that includes savannas, dense forests, and riverine areas. Key geographic features include the Ura

Hills, which offer panoramic views of the surrounding terrain, and the Tana River, which runs along the park's northern boundary. The climate is generally warm and humid, with temperatures ranging from 15°C to 30°C (59°F to 86°F). The park experiences two main rainy seasons, which support its lush vegetation and seasonal water sources. The varied topography and climate contribute to the park's ecological diversity.

Wildlife

Meru National Park is home to a wide range of wildlife species, making it a significant conservation area. The park supports populations of elephants, buffaloes, giraffes, and various antelope species, including the endangered Grevy's zebra and the rare sable antelope. Predators such as lions, leopards, and cheetahs are also present. Birdlife is abundant, with over 400 species recorded, including the African fish eagle and the white-headed vulture. The park's diverse habitats provide crucial support for both resident and migratory species.

Tourism activities

Tourism in Meru National Park offers a range of activities that highlight its natural beauty and wildlife. Game drives are a popular way to explore the park, providing opportunities to observe its diverse animal species and scenic landscapes. Bird watching is particularly rewarding due to the park's rich avian diversity. Visitors can also enjoy guided nature walks, which offer a closer look at the park's flora and fauna. Scenic viewpoints, such as those in the Ura Hills, provide excellent photo opportunities and panoramic views of the park.

Conservation efforts

Conservation efforts in Meru National Park are focused on preserving its unique biodiversity and addressing threats such as poaching and habitat degradation. The park is managed by the Kenya Wildlife Service, which works to protect its wildlife and natural resources through anti-poaching patrols, habitat management, and community outreach programs. Conservation initiatives include monitoring endangered species, promoting sustainable land use practices, and enhancing local community involvement in Conservation efforts. Research and monitoring are essential in guiding effective conservation strategies.

Accessibility and accommodation

Meru National Park is accessible by road from Nairobi, which is approximately a 5 to 6-hour drive away. The park can also be reached by flights to Meru Airport, followed by a short drive to the park. Accommodation options within the park include lodges and campsites that offer varying levels of comfort and amenities. Some lodges provide guided safari tours and additional services to enhance the visitor experience. Nearby towns such as Meru also offer additional lodging options, catering to different preferences and budgets.

Mombasa Marine National Park

Introduction

Mombasa Marine National Park, established in 1986, is a marine protected area located off the coast of Mombasa, Kenya. Covering approximately 10 square kilometers, the park is part of the larger Mombasa Marine National Reserve. It is renowned for its pristine coral reefs, diverse marine life, and beautiful coastal landscapes. The park plays a crucial role in marine conservation and offers a range of activities for visitors interested in exploring Kenya's marine environment.

Landscape and climate

The landscape of Mombasa Marine National Park is characterized by its vibrant coral reefs, clear turquoise waters, and sandy beaches. The underwater topography includes coral gardens, sea grass beds, and mangrove forests, which provide vital habitats for marine life. The climate in the area is tropical, with temperatures ranging from 24°C to

32°C (75°F to 89°F). The park experiences a bimodal rainfall pattern, with short rains from October to December and long rains from March to May, which influence the marine environment and coastal vegetation.

Wildlife

Mombasa Marine National Park is home to a diverse range of marine species. The coral reefs are teeming with colorful fish, including parrotfish, butterflyfish, and clownfish. The park also supports populations of sea turtles, such as the green turtle and hawksbill turtle, which can often be seen feeding on the reef or nesting on the nearby beaches. Dolphins are commonly spotted in the park's waters, and occasional sightings of manta rays and whales add to the park's appeal. The mangrove forests and seagrass beds are important habitats for juvenile fish and invertebrates.

Tourism activities

Tourism in Mombasa Marine National Park is focused on exploring its marine environment and enjoying its coastal beauty. Popular activities include snorkeling and scuba diving, which provide opportunities to explore the colorful coral reefs and observe diverse marine life up close. Glass-bottom boat tours offer a view of the underwater world without getting wet. Dolphin watching and boat trips are also popular. Visitors can relax on the park's sandy beaches, enjoy picnics, and take guided nature walks through the mangrove forests. The park's clear waters and rich marine biodiversity make it a favored destination for marine enthusiasts.

Conservation efforts

Conservation efforts in Mombasa Marine National Park aim to protect its coral reefs, marine life, and coastal ecosystems from threats such as pollution, overfishing, and coral bleaching. The park is managed by the Kenya Wildlife Service in collaboration with local communities and conservation organizations. Efforts include coral reef monitoring and restoration projects, marine patrols to prevent illegal fishing, and community education programs to promote sustainable practices. The park's conservation initiatives are vital for maintaining the health of its marine ecosystems and ensuring the long-term sustainability of its natural resources.

Accessibility and accommodation

Mombasa Marine National Park is easily accessible from Mombasa, which is approximately a 30-minute drive away. The park can be reached by boat from various points along the Mombasa coastline. Accommodation options near the park include a range of lodges, resorts, and guesthouses in Mombasa and the nearby coastal towns. Many lodges and resorts offer packages that include guided tours and marine activities, providing visitors with convenient access to the park and its attractions.

Mount Elgon National Park

Introduction

Mount Elgon National Park, established in 1968, is a prominent conservation area located in western Kenya, near the border with Uganda. Covering approximately 1,279 square kilometers, the park is centered around Mount Elgon, an extinct shield volcano that reaches an elevation of 4,169 meters (13,681 feet). The park is known for its diverse landscapes, rich biodiversity, and unique geological features, making it a popular destination for nature enthusiasts and hikers.

Landscape and climate

Mount Elgon National Park features a range of landscapes, from lush montane forests and bamboo groves to high-altitude moorlands and volcanic features. The park's centerpiece is Mount Elgon, which boasts a large caldera, expansive lava flows, and dramatic peaks. The climate varies with altitude, ranging from tropical and humid at lower elevations to cooler and temperate conditions at higher altitudes. Temperatures generally range from 10°C to 25°C (50°F to 77°F). The park experiences two main rainy seasons: long rains from March to May and short rains from October to December, which contribute to its lush vegetation and influence the park's hiking conditions.

Wildlife

Mount Elgon National Park is home to a diverse range of wildlife adapted to its varied environments. The park supports populations of elephants, buffaloes, and various antelope species, including the eland and duiker. It is also home to primates such as the colobus monkey and the black-and-white monkey. Birdlife is abundant, with over 300 species recorded, including the endangered lammergeier vulture, the mountain buzzard, and various sunbirds. The park's diverse habitats provide essential support for both resident and migratory species.

Tourism activities

Tourism in Mount Elgon National Park is centered around its scenic landscapes and outdoor activities. Hiking is a major attraction, with several trails offering opportunities to explore the park's diverse environments and geological features. Popular hikes include the climb to the peaks of Mount Elgon, such as the Wagagai Peak, and treks through the park's lush forests and moorlands. The park also offers bird watching, with numerous opportunities to observe its diverse avian species. Visitors can explore the park's caves, such as the Kitum Cave, which were historically used by elephants. Scenic viewpoints provide excellent opportunities for photography and appreciating the park's natural beauty.

Conservation efforts

Conservation efforts in Mount Elgon National Park focus on protecting its unique ecosystems and addressing threats such as poaching and habitat degradation. The park is managed by the Kenya

Wildlife Service in collaboration with local communities and conservation organizations. Conservation initiatives include anti-poaching measures, forest management, and habitat restoration projects. The park also engages in community outreach and education programs to promote sustainable practices and enhance local support for conservation. Research and monitoring are crucial for understanding the park's ecological dynamics and guiding effective conservation strategies.

Accessibility and accommodation

Mount Elgon National Park is accessible by road from Nairobi, approximately a 7 to 8-hour drive away. The park can also be reached from the nearby towns of Kitale and Kapchorwa, which offer access to various park entrances. Accommodation options within the park include basic lodges and campsites that offer varying levels of comfort and amenities. Some lodges provide guided tours and additional services to enhance the visitor experience. Nearby towns such as Kitale and Eldoret also offer a range of lodging options, catering to different preferences and budgets.

Mount Kenya National Park

Introduction

Mount Kenya National Park, established in 1949, is a renowned conservation area located in central Kenya. It centers around Mount Kenya, the country's highest peak and Africa's second-highest mountain, standing at 5,199 meters (17,057 feet). The park covers approximately 715 square kilometers and is celebrated for its stunning mountain landscapes, rich biodiversity, and unique ecological zones. It is a UNESCO World Heritage Site recognized for its outstanding natural beauty and ecological significance.

Landscape and climate

The landscape of Mount Kenya National Park is dominated by the towering peaks of Mount Kenya, including the main summit, Batian Peak, and the secondary peaks of Nelion and Point Lenana. The park features a diverse range of habitats, from tropical rainforests and bamboo forests at lower elevations to alpine meadows and glaciers at higher altitudes. The climate varies with altitude, with temperatures ranging from 10°C to 20°C (50°F to 68°F) at lower elevations and dropping significantly at higher altitudes. The park experiences two main rainy seasons: long rains from March to May and short rains from October to December, which contribute to the lush vegetation and influence hiking conditions.

Wildlife

Mount Kenya National Park is home to a diverse range of wildlife adapted to its varied environments. The lower slopes and forests support populations of elephants, buffaloes, and antelopes such as the bongo and the duiker. The park's high-altitude areas are home to unique species like the elusive mountain reedbuck and the endangered white-tailed mangabey. Birdlife is abundant, with over 130 species recorded, including the African crowned eagle and the rare Mount Kenya thrush. The park's diverse ecosystems provide crucial habitats for both resident and migratory species.

Tourism activities

Tourism in Mount Kenya National Park offers a range of activities that highlight its stunning landscapes and ecological diversity. Hiking and climbing are major attractions, with several trails and routes providing access to the mountain's peaks and scenic viewpoints. Popular trekking routes include the Sirimon, Naru Moru, and Chogoria routes, which lead to the summit and offer diverse experiences of the park's natural beauty. Mountaineering enthusiasts can attempt the challenging ascent to Batian Peak. The park also offers opportunities for wildlife viewing, bird watching, and nature photography. Visitors can explore the park's diverse ecological zones, from lush rainforests to alpine moorlands.

Conservation efforts

Conservation efforts in Mount Kenya National Park focus on protecting its unique ecosystems and addressing challenges such as habitat degradation, poaching, and climate change. The park is managed by the Kenya Wildlife Service in collaboration with local communities and conservation organizations. Key initiatives include anti-poaching patrols, forest management, and habitat restoration projects. The park also engages in community outreach and education programs to promote sustainable land use and conservation practices. Research and monitoring are essential for understanding the park's ecological dynamics and guiding effective conservation strategies.

Accessibility and accommodation

Mount Kenya National Park is accessible by road from Nairobi, which is approximately a 3 to 4-hour drive away. The park can also be reached from nearby towns such as Nanyuki and Meru, which offer access to various park entrances. Accommodation options within the park include lodges, campsites, and mountain huts that cater to different preferences and budgets. Some lodges and campsites offer guided trekking and climbing services. Nearby towns such as Nanyuki and Meru also provide additional lodging options and services for visitors.

Mount Longonot National Park

Introduction

Mount Longonot National Park, established in 1983, is a scenic conservation area located in the Rift Valley of Kenya. The park is centered around Mount Longonot, an extinct stratovolcano that stands at 2,776 meters (9,109 feet) above sea level. Covering an area of approximately 52 square kilometers, the park is renowned for its dramatic volcanic landscape, rich biodiversity, and panoramic views. It provides an excellent destination for those interested in geological features, wildlife, and outdoor activities.

Landscape and climate

The landscape of Mount Longonot National Park is dominated by the imposing crater of Mount Longonot, which is characterized by its steep slopes and circular caldera. The park's terrain includes diverse volcanic features, such as lava flows and cinder cones, as well as surrounding grasslands and forests. The climate is generally temperate, with temperatures ranging from 15°C to 25°C (59°F to 77°F). The park experiences a bimodal rainfall pattern, with long rains from March to May and short rains from October to December. The climate contributes to the park's varied vegetation, including grasslands and lowland forest.

Wildlife

Mount Longonot National Park supports a variety of wildlife species adapted to its volcanic and forested environments. The park is home to populations of large herbivores such as buffaloes, giraffes, and elands. Smaller mammals, including zebras and antelopes like Grant's gazelle and Thomson's gazelle, are also present. The park's avian diversity includes species such as the African hoopoe, the crowned eagle, and various sunbirds. The park's diverse habitats provide essential support for both resident and migratory species, making it a notable spot for wildlife observation.

Tourism activities

Tourism in Mount Longonot National Park revolves around exploring its volcanic features and enjoying outdoor activities. Hiking is a major attraction, with the park offering a popular trail that ascends to the summit of Mount Longonot and encircles the crater rim. The hike provides stunning panoramic views of the Rift Valley and the surrounding landscape. The park also offers opportunities for wildlife viewing, bird watching, and nature photography. The scenic beauty and unique geological features make the park a favored destination for adventure seekers and nature enthusiasts.

Conservation efforts

Conservation efforts in Mount Longonot National Park focus on preserving its unique volcanic landscape and addressing threats such as poaching and habitat degradation. The park is managed by the Kenya Wildlife Service, which implements measures to protect its wildlife and natural resources. Conservation initiatives include anti-poaching patrols, habitat restoration projects, and community outreach programs to promote sustainable practices. Research and monitoring are essential for understanding the park's ecological dynamics and guiding effective conservation strategies.

Accessibility and accommodation

Mount Longonot National Park is easily accessible by road from Nairobi, which is approximately a 1.5 to 2-hour drive away. The park is located near the town of Naivasha, which provides access to the park's main entrance. Accommodation options near the park include lodges, guesthouses, and campsites in Naivasha and its surrounding areas. These options offer varying levels of comfort and amenities and provide convenient access to the park and its attractions. Visitors can also explore nearby attractions such as Lake Naivasha and Hell's Gate National Park.

Nairobi National Park

Introduction

Nairobi National Park, established in 1946, is a unique wildlife sanctuary located just 7 kilometers (4 miles) from the bustling city center of Nairobi, Kenya's capital. Covering an area of approximately 117 square kilometers, the park is renowned for its proximity to an urban environment and its diverse range of wildlife. It serves as a crucial conservation area and an accessible destination for both locals and tourists, offering a unique opportunity to experience wildlife close to a major city.

Landscape and climate

The landscape of Nairobi National Park features a mix of savanna, grasslands, and scattered acacia woodlands. The park's topography includes gentle hills, riverine vegetation along the Nairobi River, and a series of wetlands and swamps that provide important water sources for wildlife. The climate is generally mild, with temperatures ranging from 10°C to 26°C (50°F to 79°F). Nairobi National Park experiences two main rainy seasons: the long rains from March to May and the short rains from October to December. The climate supports a range of habitats and seasonal changes in vegetation.

Wildlife

Despite its proximity to Nairobi, the park is home to a surprising variety of wildlife. It supports populations of iconic African species such as lions, giraffes, zebras, and rhinoceroses, including both black and white rhinos. The park is also home to buffaloes, elands, and various antelope species. Predators such as cheetahs and hyenas are present, and over 400 bird species have been recorded, including the African fish eagle, secretary bird, and numerous waterfowl. The park's diverse habitats provide essential support for its wildlife and contribute to its ecological significance.

Tourism activities

Tourism in Nairobi National Park offers a range of activities that highlight its unique location and wildlife. Game drives are a popular way to explore the park and observe its diverse animal species. The park is also known for its excellent bird watching opportunities, with numerous species easily spotted. Visitors can explore the park's trails and enjoy guided walking safaris, which provide a closer look at the park's flora and fauna. The Nairobi Animal Orphanage and the David Sheldrick Wildlife Trust's Elephant Orphanage, located nearby, offer additional attractions and educational experiences related to wildlife conservation.

Conservation efforts

Conservation efforts in Nairobi National Park focus on protecting its wildlife and maintaining the integrity of its ecosystems in the face of urbanization and development pressures. The park is managed by the Kenya Wildlife Service, which implements anti-poaching measures, habitat management, and wildlife monitoring programs. Conservation initiatives also include community outreach and education programs to promote coexistence between urban populations and wildlife. The park plays a vital role in conservation education and raising awareness about the importance of protecting natural habitats.

Accessibility and accommodation

Nairobi National Park is easily accessible from Nairobi, with the main entrance located just a short drive from the city center. The park can be reached by private car, taxi, or guided tour. Although there are no accommodation facilities within the park itself, there are numerous lodging options in Nairobi and its surrounding areas. These include hotels, lodges, and guesthouses that cater to various preferences and budgets. Many accommodations in Nairobi offer safari packages that include guided tours of the park, providing visitors with convenient access to its attractions.

Ol Donyo Sabuk National Park

Introduction

Ol Donyo Sabuk National Park, established in 1967, is a serene and less-visited conservation area located in central Kenya, about 85 kilometers (53 miles) northeast of Nairobi. The park is centered around Ol Donyo Sabuk, a prominent mountain peak rising to 2,146 meters (7,041 feet) above sea level. Covering an area of approximately 60 square kilometers, the park is known for its scenic beauty, diverse wildlife, and important water catchment areas, making it a key ecological zone in the region.

Landscape and climate

The landscape of Ol Donyo Sabuk National Park is dominated by the distinctive peak of Ol Donyo Sabuk, which provides dramatic views and a prominent feature in the park. The terrain includes a variety of habitats, such as rocky outcrops, dense forests, and open grasslands. The park's vegetation varies with altitude, ranging from lower montane forests to high-altitude moorlands. The climate is generally temperate, with temperatures ranging from 15°C to 25°C (59°F to 77°F). The park experiences two main rainy seasons: long rains from March to May and short rains from October to December. This climate supports a range of plant and animal species and influences the park's seasonal dynamics.

Wildlife

Ol Donyo Sabuk National Park supports a variety of wildlife adapted to its diverse habitats. The park is home to several species of large mammals, including elephants, buffaloes, and giraffes. Predators such as lions and leopards are also present, although they are less commonly seen. The park's smaller mammal species include zebras, antelopes such as the Grant's gazelle, and various primates. Birdlife is abundant, with species like the African harrier-hawk, the White-cheeked turaco, and various raptors. The park's forested and open areas provide crucial habitats for both resident and migratory species.

Tourism activities

Tourism in Ol Donyo Sabuk National Park is centered around its scenic landscapes and opportunities for outdoor activities. Hiking is a major attraction, with trails leading to the summit of Ol Donyo Sabuk and offering panoramic views of the surrounding landscape. The park's diverse habitats provide excellent opportunities for wildlife viewing, bird watching, and nature photography. Guided nature walks allow visitors to explore the park's flora and fauna up close. The park's relatively low visitor numbers contribute to a more tranquil and immersive experience compared to some of Kenya's more frequented national parks.

Conservation efforts

Conservation efforts in Ol Donyo Sabuk National Park focus on preserving its unique ecosystems and managing human-wildlife interactions. The park is managed by the Kenya Wildlife Service, which implements measures to protect wildlife and natural resources. Conservation initiatives include anti-poaching efforts, habitat management, and community engagement programs. The park's status as an important water catchment area also underscores the need for effective management of its natural resources. Research and monitoring activities contribute to understanding the park's ecological dynamics and guiding conservation strategies.

Accessibility and accommodation

Ol Donyo Sabuk National Park is accessible by road from Nairobi, which is approximately a 1.5 to 2-hour drive away. The park can be reached via the town of Thika, with a well-maintained road leading to the park entrance. While there are no accommodation facilities within the park itself, visitors can find lodging options in nearby towns such as Thika and Nairobi. These accommodations range from budget guesthouses to mid-range lodges and hotels. Many of these establishments offer guided tours and transport services to the park, providing convenient access for visitors.

Ruma National Park

Introduction

Ruma National Park, established in 1966, is a relatively remote and unique conservation area located in western Kenya, near the border with Uganda. Covering approximately 120 square kilometers, the park is renowned for its rugged landscapes and its role as a refuge for the endangered Rothschild's giraffe. The park provides a vital sanctuary for various species and is known for its picturesque scenery and rich biodiversity.

Landscape and climate

The landscape of Ruma National Park is characterized by a mix of rolling hills, grasslands, and scattered acacia trees. The terrain includes rocky outcrops and seasonal riverbeds, which add to the park's rugged beauty. The climate is generally warm and semi-arid, with temperatures ranging from 20°C to 30°C (68°F to 86°F). The park experiences a bimodal rainfall pattern, with long rains from March to May and short rains from October to December. The climate supports a variety of plant species and influences the seasonal availability of water and vegetation.

Wildlife

Ruma National Park is home to a range of wildlife species adapted to its semi-arid environment. One of the park's major highlights is the Rothschild's giraffe, an endangered subspecies that is the focus of significant Conservation efforts. Other large mammals present in the park include buffaloes, elands, and various antelope species such as Grant's gazelle and impalas. Predators such as lions and hyenas are also found in the park, although sightings can be less frequent. The park's birdlife is diverse, with over 400 species recorded, including the rare and beautiful lilac-breasted roller, the white-headed vulture, and various raptors.

Tourism activities

Tourism in Ruma National Park offers a range of activities centered around its wildlife and scenic landscapes. Game drives are a popular way to explore the park and observe its diverse animal species. Bird watching is another key activity, with opportunities to spot a wide variety of avian species. The park's relatively low visitor numbers provide a more tranquil and intimate wildlife experience compared to some of Kenya's more frequented parks. Guided nature walks and hiking opportunities allow visitors to explore the park's flora and enjoy its scenic beauty up close.

Conservation efforts

Conservation efforts in Ruma National Park focus on protecting its unique wildlife and preserving its natural habitats. The park is managed by the Kenya Wildlife Service, which implements measures to combat poaching and manage wildlife populations. Conservation initiatives include anti-poaching patrols, habitat restoration projects, and community outreach programs to promote sustainable practices.

The park's role as a sanctuary for the endangered Rothschild's giraffe is a key focus, with ongoing efforts to monitor and support the giraffe population. Research and monitoring activities are essential for understanding the park's ecological dynamics and guiding conservation strategies.

Accessibility and accommodation

Ruma National Park is accessible by road from Nairobi, which is approximately a 6 to 7-hour drive away. The park can also be reached from the town of Homa Bay, which is closer and provides access to the park's entrance. While there are no accommodation facilities within the park itself, visitors can find lodging options in nearby towns such as Homa Bay and Kisumu. These accommodations range from budget guesthouses to mid-range lodges and hotels. Many of these establishments offer guided tours and transport services to the park, providing convenient access for visitors.

Saiwa Swamp National Park

Introduction

Saiwa Swamp National Park, established in 1974, is a small but significant conservation area located in western Kenya, near the town of Kitale. Covering an area of approximately 3.8 square kilometers, the park is renowned for its unique swampy terrain and rich biodiversity. It plays a crucial role in protecting the endangered Sitatunga antelope and serves as an important sanctuary for various other wildlife species and birdlife.

Landscape and climate

The landscape of Saiwa Swamp National Park is characterized by its extensive swampy areas, wetlands, and dense vegetation. The park's terrain includes marshes, papyrus reeds, and small forested areas, creating a diverse and intricate ecosystem. The climate is generally temperate, with temperatures ranging from 15°C to 25°C (59°F to 77°F). The park experiences two main rainy seasons: the long rains from March to May and the short rains from October to December.

The swampy conditions and seasonal variations in water levels significantly influence the park's flora and fauna.

Wildlife

Saiwa Swamp National Park is home to a variety of wildlife adapted to its wetland environment. The park is best known for its population of Sitatunga antelopes, a swamp-dwelling species that is highly adapted to life in marshy conditions. Other mammal species in the park include the bushbuck, duiker, and occasionally elephants and buffaloes that venture into the swampy areas. The park's avian diversity is notable, with over 400 bird species recorded, including the rare and elusive papyrus gonolek, the black-headed heron, and various waterfowl. The swamp's rich vegetation supports a diverse array of insects and amphibians.

Tourism activities

Tourism in Saiwa Swamp National Park offers unique opportunities to explore its wetland environment and observe its specialized wildlife. Walking safaris are a major attraction, allowing visitors to traverse the park's swampy trails and view wildlife up close. The park's boardwalks and observation platforms provide excellent vantage points for bird watching and nature photography. Guided tours offer insights into the park's ecology and the behavior of its resident species. Due to its compact size, the park provides a more intimate and serene wildlife experience compared to larger national parks.

Conservation efforts

Conservation efforts in Saiwa Swamp National Park focus on protecting its fragile wetland ecosystems and supporting its wildlife populations. The park is managed by the Kenya Wildlife Service, which implements measures to prevent poaching and manage habitat degradation. Conservation initiatives include habitat restoration projects, anti-poaching patrols, and community engagement programs aimed at promoting sustainable practices. Research and monitoring activities are essential for understanding the park's ecological dynamics and guiding effective conservation strategies, particularly for the endangered Sitatunga antelope.

Accessibility and accommodation

Saiwa Swamp National Park is accessible by road from Nairobi, which is approximately a 6 to 7-hour drive away. The park can also be reached from Kitale, which is closer and provides access to the park's entrance. While there are no accommodation facilities within the park itself, visitors can find lodging options in Kitale and its surrounding areas. These accommodations range from budget guesthouses to mid-range lodges and hotels. Many of these establishments offer guided tours and transport services to the park, providing convenient access for visitors.

Sibiloi National Park

Introduction

Sibiloi National Park, established in 1973, is a remote and unique conservation area located in the northern part of Kenya, near the shores of Lake Turkana. Covering an area of approximately 1,570 square kilometers, the park is renowned for its arid landscapes, rich archaeological sites, and diverse wildlife. It plays a crucial role in preserving the cultural and natural heritage of the region and offers a distinctive experience for adventurous travelers.

Landscape and climate

The landscape of Sibiloi National Park is characterized by its arid and semi-arid terrain, featuring rugged hills, volcanic formations, and expansive plains. The park's terrain includes the impressive Sibiloi Mountain, which rises prominently in the landscape, and the shores of Lake Turkana, which provide a vital water source for the park's wildlife. The climate is hot and arid, with temperatures ranging from 20°C to 40°C (68°F to 104°F). The park experiences minimal rainfall, with most of it occurring between April and September. The harsh climate influences the park's vegetation, which consists mainly of hardy, drought-resistant plant species.

Wildlife

Sibiloi National Park is home to a variety of wildlife adapted to its arid environment. The park's mammalian fauna includes species such as the reticulated giraffe, Grevy's zebra, and various antelope species like the Beisa oryx and Grant's gazelle. Predators such as lions and hyenas are present, although sightings can be less frequent due to the park's vast and open terrain. The park's avian diversity includes species such as the African fish eagle, secretary bird, and several species of raptors. The park's diverse habitats support a range of wildlife and contribute to its ecological significance.

Tourism activities

Tourism in Sibiloi National Park offers a range of activities centered around its unique landscapes and archaeological significance. Game drives provide opportunities to explore the park's diverse wildlife and enjoy its dramatic scenery. Bird watching is another key activity, with numerous species to observe, especially around Lake Turkana. The park is also known for its archaeological sites, including ancient fossils and early human artifacts, which attract researchers and history enthusiasts. The park's remote location and harsh conditions make it ideal for those seeking an adventurous and off-the-beaten-path experience.

Conservation efforts

Conservation efforts in Sibiloi National Park focus on preserving its unique ecosystems, protecting its wildlife, and managing human impacts. The park is managed by the Kenya Wildlife Service, which implements measures to prevent poaching and manage habitat degradation. Conservation initiatives include monitoring wildlife populations, habitat restoration projects, and research activities to understand the park's ecological dynamics. The park's archaeological sites are also protected and studied to preserve their historical significance. Community outreach and education programs aim to promote sustainable practices and support Conservation efforts.

Accessibility and accommodation

Sibiloi National Park is accessible by road from Nairobi, which is approximately a 12 to 14-hour drive away, depending on road conditions. The park can also be reached by chartered flights from Nairobi to Lokichoggio, followed by a road transfer to the park. Due to its remote location, visitors should be well-prepared for the journey. Accommodation options within the park are limited, and visitors typically stay in basic campsites or lodges in nearby towns such as Loyangalani. These accommodations offer basic facilities and provide access to the park's attractions. Advance bookings and proper travel arrangements are recommended for a smooth visit.

South Island National Park

Introduction

South Island National Park, located in Lake Victoria, is a unique and relatively lesser-known conservation area in Kenya. Established in 1983, the park covers South Island on Lake Victoria and is known for its rich biodiversity and scenic beauty. The park's establishment aimed to protect the island's natural habitats and provide a sanctuary for various wildlife species. It offers a tranquil escape for those interested in exploring Kenya's freshwater ecosystems and diverse avian life.

Landscape and climate

South Island National Park features a predominantly flat and forested landscape with a mix of dense vegetation, grasslands, and wetlands. The island's terrain is characterized by its lush vegetation and proximity to Lake Victoria, which influences the park's environment. The climate is typically tropical, with temperatures ranging from 22°C to 30°C (72°F to 86°F). The park experiences two main rainy seasons: the long rains from March to May and the short rains from October to December. The proximity to Lake Victoria provides a humid environment that supports a variety of plant and animal species.

Wildlife

South Island National Park is known for its diverse wildlife, particularly its avian population. The park is an important habitat for various bird species, including the endangered Madagascar fish eagle and numerous waterfowl. The island also supports populations of smaller mammals such as monkeys and various rodent species. While large mammals are less common, the park's wetlands and forests provide crucial habitats for its resident species. The lake environment supports aquatic life, including fish and amphibians that contribute to the island's ecological balance.

Tourism activities

Tourism in South Island National Park primarily revolves around its avian diversity and scenic beauty. Bird watching is a major activity, with opportunities to observe a wide range of bird species, including rare and migratory birds. The park's lush vegetation and tranquil setting make it an ideal destination for nature walks and photography. Boat tours around the island and along Lake Victoria provide unique perspectives of the park's landscape and wildlife. Visitors can also engage in educational activities related to the park's ecosystems and Conservation efforts.

Conservation efforts

Conservation efforts in South Island National Park focus on preserving its unique habitats and protecting its wildlife. The park is managed by the Kenya Wildlife Service, which implements measures to prevent poaching and habitat degradation. Conservation initiatives include habitat restoration projects, monitoring of bird populations, and research activities to understand the park's ecological dynamics. The park's location on Lake Victoria highlights the importance of maintaining water quality and protecting aquatic habitats. Community engagement and education programs aim to promote sustainable practices and support Conservation efforts.

Accessibility and accommodation

South Island National Park is accessible by boat from various points around Lake Victoria. The park can be reached from Kisumu, which is approximately 50 kilometers (31 miles) away by boat. Visitors typically travel to Kisumu and arrange boat transfers to the island. Accommodation options on the island are limited, and visitors often stay in lodges or guesthouses in Kisumu or nearby towns. These accommodations range from budget options to more comfortable lodges, providing access to the park and its attractions. Advance bookings and proper travel arrangements are recommended for a smooth visit.

Tsavo East National Park

Introduction

Tsavo East National Park, one of Kenya's largest and most renowned wildlife reserves, was established in 1948 and covers approximately 13,747 square kilometers. Located in southeastern Kenya, the park is part of the larger Tsavo Conservation Area, which also includes Tsavo West National Park. Known for its vast, open plains and diverse wildlife, Tsavo East is a key destination for those seeking an authentic safari experience in Kenya. The park plays a crucial role in conserving a wide array of species and protecting critical habitats.

Landscape and climate

Tsavo East National Park features a varied landscape of expansive savannas, semi-arid plains, and scattered volcanic hills. The terrain includes rocky outcrops and seasonal rivers, such as the Galana River, which provides a vital water source for wildlife. The park's vegetation is predominantly thorny acacia woodland and scrub, with patches of grasslands. The climate is typically hot and dry, with temperatures ranging from 20°C to 35°C (68°F to 95°F). The park experiences two main rainy seasons: the long rains from March to May and the short rains from October to December. The seasonal rains influence the park's flora and the availability of water for wildlife.

Wildlife

Tsavo East National Park is renowned for its diverse wildlife, including large populations of iconic African species. The park is home to significant numbers of elephants, including the famous "maneless" lions. Other large mammals include buffaloes, giraffes, and various antelope species such as the Grant's gazelle and impala. Predators like lions, leopards, and cheetahs can be found in the park, although sightings may require some patience due to the vast expanse. Birdlife is abundant, with over 500 species recorded, including raptors such as the African fish eagle and various hornbills. The park's rivers and wetlands support a range of aquatic species and provide vital water sources for wildlife.

Tourism activities

Tourism in Tsavo East National Park focuses on its wildlife and expansive landscapes. Game drives are the primary activity, allowing visitors to explore the park's vast plains and observe its diverse wildlife. The park's large size and open terrain provide excellent opportunities for wildlife viewing and photography. Bird watching is also popular, with numerous species to observe throughout the park. The park offers several scenic spots, such as the Yatta Plateau and the Lugard Falls, which provide unique perspectives of the landscape. Guided walks and cultural tours can be arranged to enhance the visitor experience and provide insights into the park's natural and cultural heritage.

Conservation efforts

Conservation efforts in Tsavo East National Park focus on protecting its diverse wildlife and managing its extensive habitats. The park is managed by the Kenya Wildlife Service, which implements measures to prevent poaching and manage human-wildlife conflicts. Key conservation initiatives include anti-poaching patrols, habitat management projects, and community outreach programs. The park's role as a sanctuary for large populations of elephants and other wildlife highlights the importance of ongoing Conservation efforts. Research and monitoring activities are essential for understanding the park's ecological dynamics and guiding effective management strategies.

Accessibility and accommodation

Tsavo East National Park is accessible by road from Nairobi, which is approximately a 5 to 6-hour drive away, depending on road conditions. The park can also be reached from the coastal town of Mombasa, which is about a 3 to 4-hour drive. There are several entry points into the park, with the main gates being the Voi Gate and the Sala Gate. Accommodation options within the park include lodges and tented camps, ranging from budget to mid-range options. Some well-known lodges include the Voi Safari Lodge and the Ashnil Aruba Lodge. Additional accommodation options are available in nearby towns such as Voi and Tsavo.

Tsavo West National Park

Introduction

Tsavo West National Park, established in 1948, is one of Kenya's premier wildlife reserves and is part of the Tsavo Conservation Area, alongside Tsavo East National Park. Covering approximately 9,065 square kilometers, the park is renowned for its diverse landscapes, abundant wildlife, and rich ecological history. Tsavo West offers a contrasting experience to its eastern counterpart, with its lush vegetation and dramatic scenery, making it a popular destination for wildlife enthusiasts and adventure seekers.

Landscape and climate

Tsavo West National Park features a varied landscape that includes volcanic hills, rugged terrain, and lush vegetation. Notable geographical features include the Mzima Springs, a series of crystal-clear springs that provide vital water sources for the park's wildlife, and the Shetani Lava Flow, a volcanic formation that adds to the park's dramatic scenery. The park's terrain includes savannas, dense thickets, and riverine forests. The climate is typically warm and semi-arid, with temperatures ranging from 20°C to 30°C (68°F to

86°F). The park experiences two main rainy seasons: the long rains from March to May and the short rains from October to December. The seasonal rains influence the park's vegetation and water availability.

Wildlife

Tsavo West National Park is renowned for its rich wildlife diversity. The park is home to large populations of elephants, including the iconic "maneless" lions. Other notable species include buffaloes, giraffes, and various antelope species such as the Grant's gazelle and the impala. Predators such as lions, leopards, and hyenas are also present, and the park's diverse habitats support a range of other mammals. Birdlife is abundant, with over 500 species recorded, including the rare and elusive Vulturine guineafowl and various raptors. The park's water sources, such as Mzima Springs, support aquatic life, including hippos and crocodiles.

Tourism activities

Tourism in Tsavo West National Park offers a range of activities centered around its diverse landscapes and wildlife. Game drives are a popular way to explore the park and view its wildlife, with opportunities to see the "maneless" lions and other iconic species. The park's scenic spots, such as the Mzima Springs and the Shetani Lava Flow, provide unique sightseeing opportunities. Bird watching is another key activity, with numerous species to observe throughout the park. Guided walks and nature hikes offer a chance to explore the park's flora and learn about its ecological systems. The park's relatively remote and less frequented nature provides a more serene and intimate wildlife experience.

Conservation efforts

Conservation efforts in Tsavo West National Park focus on protecting its diverse wildlife and managing its complex ecosystems. The park is managed by the Kenya Wildlife Service, which implements measures to combat poaching and mitigate human-wildlife conflicts. Conservation initiatives include anti-poaching patrols, habitat restoration projects, and community engagement programs. The protection of water sources, such as Mzima Springs, is crucial for sustaining wildlife populations. Research and monitoring activities help to understand the park's ecological dynamics and guide conservation strategies. Community outreach programs aim to foster positive relationships between local communities and Conservation efforts.

Accessibility and accommodation

Tsavo West National Park is accessible by road from Nairobi, which is approximately a 5 to 6-hour drive away, depending on road conditions. The park can also be reached from the coastal town of Mombasa, which is about a 3 to 4-hour drive. The main entry points into the park include the Tsavo Gate and the Mtito Andei Gate. Accommodation options within the park include lodges and tented camps, offering a range of options from budget to mid-range. Notable lodges include the Kilaguni Serena Safari Lodge and the Finch Hattons Luxury Tented Camp. Additional accommodation options are available in nearby towns such as Voi and Mtito Andei.

Watamu Marine National Park

Introduction

Watamu Marine National Park, established in 1968, is one of Kenya's premier marine protected areas located along the Indian Ocean coast near the town of Watamu. Covering approximately 10 square kilometers, the park is renowned for its vibrant coral reefs, diverse marine life, and pristine coastal habitats. It plays a vital role in conserving marine ecosystems and provides exceptional opportunities for snorkeling, diving, and marine tourism.

Landscape and climate

Watamu Marine National Park features a stunning coastal landscape with crystal-clear waters, extensive coral reefs, and sandy beaches. The park's underwater landscape includes colorful coral gardens, sea grass beds, and tidal lagoons. The climate is tropical, with temperatures ranging from 25°C to 30°C (77°F to 86°F) throughout the year. The park experiences two main rainy seasons: the long rains from April to May and the short rains from October to December. The climate and warm ocean waters contribute to the park's rich marine biodiversity and support various aquatic ecosystems.

Wildlife

Watamu Marine National Park is home to a diverse array of marine species. The park's coral reefs provide essential habitats for a wide variety of fish, including butterflyfish, clownfish, and parrotfish. The park is also known for its populations of sea turtles, including the green turtle and the hawksbill turtle, which use the park's beaches for nesting. Marine mammals such as dolphins and occasional sightings of whales add to the park's appeal. The park's mangroves and seagrass beds support numerous invertebrates and provide breeding grounds for various marine species.

Tourism activities

Tourism in Watamu Marine National Park focuses on its marine and coastal attractions. Snorkeling and scuba diving are popular activities, allowing visitors to explore the vibrant coral reefs and observe a variety of marine life. The park offers guided tours for both activities, providing insights into the marine ecosystems and ensuring safety. Glass-bottom boat tours provide an excellent way to view the underwater world without getting wet. The park's beaches are ideal for relaxation, sunbathing, and swimming. Visitors can also enjoy bird watching, as the coastal area is home to various seabird species.

Conservation efforts

Conservation efforts in Watamu Marine National Park are crucial for preserving its marine and coastal ecosystems. The park is managed by the Kenya Wildlife Service (KWS) in collaboration with local communities and conservation organizations. Key conservation initiatives include the protection of coral reefs, monitoring of marine species, and management of human activities to reduce environmental impact. The park also engages in research activities to understand and address threats to marine ecosystems. Community outreach programs promote sustainable practices and involve local communities in Conservation efforts, enhancing their role in protecting the park's natural resources.

Accessibility and accommodation

Watamu Marine National Park is accessible by road from Nairobi, which is approximately a 6 to 7-hour drive away, depending on traffic and road conditions. The park can also be reached from Mombasa, which is about a 2-hour drive. The town of Watamu serves as the main gateway to the park, with several entry points along the coast. Accommodation options in and around Watamu include a range of lodges, resorts, and guesthouses, catering to various budgets. Some well-known lodges include the Hemingways Watamu and the Turtle Bay Beach Club. Many accommodations offer easy access to the park and can arrange tours and activities for visitors.

Kenyan game reserves

Maasai Mara National Reserve

Introduction

Maasai Mara National Reserve, often simply referred to as the Maasai Mara, is one of Kenya's most iconic and celebrated wildlife reserves. Established in 1961, it covers approximately 1,510 square kilometers and is renowned for its exceptional wildlife viewing and dramatic landscapes. Located in southwestern Kenya, adjacent to the Serengeti National Park in Tanzania, the Maasai Mara is famous for its annual Great Migration, where millions of wildebeest, zebras, and gazelles traverse the plains in search of fresh grazing.

Landscape and climate

The Maasai Mara features a varied landscape of rolling savannahs, acacia woodlands, and riverine forests. The rolling plains are punctuated by occasional hills and rocky outcrops, such as the Mara River, which provides a vital water source for wildlife. The climate is typically temperate with temperatures ranging from 15°C to 25°C (59°F to 77°F) during the day and cooler temperatures at night. The reserve experiences two main rainy seasons: the long rains from March to May and the short rains from October to December. These rains significantly influence the reserve's vegetation and wildlife movements, particularly during the Great Migration.

Wildlife

The Maasai Mara is renowned for its rich biodiversity and large concentrations of wildlife. It is home to the "Big Five" (lion, leopard, elephant, buffalo, and rhinoceros) and offers excellent opportunities to observe these iconic species. The reserve is particularly famous for its large populations of lions and cheetahs. During the Great Migration, the park hosts one of the most spectacular wildlife events on the planet, with thousands of wildebeest, zebras, and gazelles crossing the Mara River. The reserve also supports a range of other mammals, including giraffes, hippos, and hyenas, as well as over 450 bird species, such as the Secretary bird and the African Fish Eagle.

Tourism activities

Tourism in Maasai Mara National Reserve is centered around its wildlife and breathtaking landscapes. Game drives are the primary activity, providing visitors with opportunities to see the Big Five and witness the Great Migration. Hot air balloon safaris offer a unique aerial perspective of the reserve and its wildlife, followed by a celebratory champagne breakfast. Bird watching is popular, with numerous species to observe throughout the year. Cultural visits to Maasai villages provide insights into the local Maasai community's traditions and way of life. The reserve also offers walking safaris and night drives, which add to the diverse experiences available.

Conservation efforts

Conservation efforts in Maasai Mara National Reserve focus on protecting its diverse wildlife and managing its extensive ecosystems. The reserve is managed by the Kenya Wildlife Service in collaboration with local Maasai communities and conservation organizations. Key initiatives include anti-poaching measures, habitat management, and community conservation programs. Efforts to address human-wildlife conflicts and promote sustainable land use are integral to preserving the reserve's ecological balance. Research and monitoring activities help inform conservation strategies and ensure the protection of key species and habitats.

Accessibility and accommodation

Maasai Mara National Reserve is accessible by road and air. It is approximately a 5 to 6-hour drive from Nairobi, depending on road conditions and the entry point used. Alternatively, visitors can fly from Nairobi to one of the many airstrips in the reserve, with flight times typically ranging from 45 minutes to 1 hour. Accommodation within the reserve includes a range of options, from luxury lodges and tented camps to more budget-friendly campsites. Some well-known lodges include the Mara Serena Safari Lodge and the Governors' Camp. Many accommodations offer game drives and other safari activities, providing a full experience of the reserve's wildlife and landscapes.

Samburu National Reserve

Introduction

Samburu National Reserve is a renowned wildlife sanctuary located in northern Kenya, established in 1962. Covering approximately 165 square kilometers, the reserve is situated along the banks of the Ewaso Ng'iro River, which provides a vital water source for its diverse wildlife. Samburu is celebrated for its unique combination of arid landscapes, specialized wildlife, and rich cultural heritage. The reserve offers a distinctive safari experience, characterized by its semi-desert environment and the opportunity to see rare and endemic species.

Landscape and climate

The landscape of Samburu National Reserve is defined by its arid and semi-arid terrain, featuring open savannahs, acacia woodlands, and rugged hills. The Ewaso Ng'iro River, which flows through the reserve, is a crucial water source that supports a variety of wildlife and vegetation. The park's terrain includes rocky outcrops and seasonal floodplains. The climate is generally hot and dry, with temperatures ranging from 20°C to 35°C (68°F to 95°F). Samburu experiences two main rainy seasons: the long rains from March to May and the short rains from October to December. The dry conditions contribute to the reserve's distinctive ecosystem and wildlife adaptations.

Wildlife

Samburu National Reserve is known for its unique and specialized wildlife. The reserve is one of the best places to see the "Samburu Special Five," which includes the reticulated giraffe, Grevy's zebra, Somali ostrich, Beisa oryx, and the gerenuk. These species are adapted to the arid conditions of the reserve and are less commonly found in other parts of Kenya. Samburu is also home to large populations of elephants, lions, leopards, and cheetahs. The reserve's diverse birdlife includes over 350 species, such as the African fish eagle and the vibrant lilac-breasted roller. The Ewaso Ng'iro River supports aquatic species, including hippos and crocodiles.

Tourism activities

Tourism in Samburu National Reserve revolves around its unique wildlife and stunning landscapes. Game drives are the primary activity, offering visitors opportunities to see the "Samburu Special Five" and other wildlife species. The riverbanks and open plains provide excellent spots for wildlife viewing and photography. Bird watching is popular, with numerous species to observe throughout the year. Cultural visits to nearby Samburu communities allow visitors to learn about the traditions and lifestyle of the local Samburu people. Guided nature walks and night drives offer additional ways to explore the reserve and experience its diverse environments.

Conservation efforts

Conservation efforts in Samburu National Reserve focus on preserving its unique ecosystems and protecting its specialized wildlife. The reserve is managed by the Kenya Wildlife Service in collaboration with local communities and conservation organizations. Key conservation initiatives include anti-poaching measures, habitat restoration projects, and the protection of water sources like the Ewaso Ng'iro River. Community-based conservation programs involve local communities in wildlife protection and sustainable land use practices. Research and monitoring activities help to track wildlife populations and inform conservation strategies. Efforts to mitigate human-wildlife conflicts and promote sustainable tourism are integral to the reserve's conservation success.

Accessibility and accommodation

Samburu National Reserve is accessible by road and air. It is approximately a 5 to 6-hour drive from Nairobi, depending on road conditions and traffic. The reserve can also be reached by scheduled flights from Nairobi to the nearby Samburu airstrip, with flight times typically ranging from 1 hour to 1 hour 30 minutes. Accommodation options within and around the reserve include a range of lodges and tented camps, from luxury to mid-range. Notable lodges include the Samburu Intrepids Camp and the Sarova Shaba Game Lodge. Many accommodations offer game drives, guided walks, and cultural activities, providing a comprehensive safari experience.

Buffalo Springs National Reserve

Introduction

Buffalo Springs National Reserve is a picturesque wildlife reserve located in northern Kenya, established in 1948. Covering approximately 131 square kilometers, the reserve is situated adjacent to Samburu National Reserve, separated by the Ewaso Ng'iro River. Known for its scenic beauty and diverse wildlife, Buffalo Springs provides a vital sanctuary for both flora and fauna in the arid and semi-arid regions of Kenya. The reserve is named after the Buffalo Springs, a natural spring that provides a crucial water source for the reserve's wildlife.

Landscape and climate

The landscape of Buffalo Springs National Reserve features a mix of open savannahs, acacia woodlands, and rocky outcrops. The Ewaso Ng'iro River, which flows along the southern boundary of the reserve, provides a key water source and supports lush vegetation along its banks. The terrain includes rolling hills and floodplains that add to the park's scenic beauty. The climate is generally hot and dry, with temperatures ranging from 20°C to 35°C (68°F to 95°F). The reserve experiences two main rainy seasons: the long rains from March to May and the short rains from October to December. These seasonal rains influence the park's vegetation and wildlife movements, providing temporary relief during the dry periods.

Wildlife

Buffalo Springs National Reserve is home to a variety of wildlife adapted to the arid conditions. The reserve is known for its populations of elephants, lions, leopards, and cheetahs. Buffalo Springs also supports a range of antelope species, including Grant's gazelle, impala, and oryx. The Ewaso Ng'iro River attracts large numbers of hippos and crocodiles. Birdlife in the reserve is diverse, with over 350 species recorded, such as the African fish eagle and the beautiful lilac-breasted roller. The reserve's varied habitats support a range of other species, including hyenas, giraffes, and warthogs.

Tourism activities

Tourism in Buffalo Springs National Reserve focuses on wildlife viewing and exploring its scenic landscapes. Game drives are the primary activity, offering opportunities to observe the reserve's diverse wildlife and enjoy its picturesque scenery. The riverbanks and floodplains provide excellent spots for wildlife photography and observation. Bird watching is popular, with numerous species to spot throughout the year. Cultural visits to nearby Samburu communities allow visitors to learn about the local Maasai and Samburu cultures. Guided nature walks and night drives offer additional ways to experience the reserve's natural beauty and wildlife.

Conservation efforts

Conservation efforts in Buffalo Springs National Reserve aim to protect its unique ecosystems and wildlife. The reserve is managed by the Kenya Wildlife Service (KWS) in collaboration with local communities and conservation organizations. Key initiatives include anti-poaching measures, habitat management, and the protection of water sources such as the Buffalo Springs. Community-based conservation programs involve local communities in wildlife protection and sustainable land use practices. Research and monitoring activities help track wildlife populations and inform conservation strategies. Efforts to address human-wildlife conflicts and promote eco-friendly tourism practices are integral to the reserve's conservation success.

Accessibility and accommodation

Buffalo Springs National Reserve is accessible by road and air. It is approximately a 5 to 6-hour drive from Nairobi, depending on road conditions and traffic. The reserve can also be reached by scheduled flights from Nairobi to the nearby airstrip, with flight times typically ranging from 1 hour to 1 hour 30 minutes. Accommodation options within and around the reserve include a range of lodges and tented camps, from mid-range to luxury. Notable lodges include the Buffalo Springs Lodge and the Sarova Shaba Game Lodge, which also serves as a base for exploring the adjacent Samburu National Reserve. Many accommodations offer game drives, guided walks, and other safari activities, providing a comprehensive wildlife experience.

Shaba National Reserve

Introduction

Shaba National Reserve is a captivating wildlife reserve located in northern Kenya, established in 1967. Covering approximately 239 square kilometers, the reserve is situated in the semi-arid region near the Ewaso Ng'iro River. Shaba is renowned for its distinctive landscapes, diverse wildlife, and unique ecosystems. It forms part of the larger Shaba, Samburu, and Buffalo Springs ecosystem, often collectively referred to as the "Shaba Complex." The reserve offers a remote and unspoiled safari experience, characterized by its rugged terrain and rich cultural heritage.

Landscape and climate

The landscape of Shaba National Reserve is characterized by its arid and semi-arid environment, featuring dramatic hills, rugged outcrops, and open savannahs. The reserve is traversed by the Ewaso Ng'iro River, which supports lush vegetation along its banks and provides a vital water source for the wildlife. The terrain includes rocky hills, floodplains, and seasonal wetlands. The climate is hot and dry, with temperatures ranging from 20°C to 35°C (68°F to 95°F). Shaba experiences two main rainy seasons: the long rains from March to May and the short rains from October to December. The dry conditions and seasonal rains significantly influence the reserve's vegetation and wildlife movements.

Wildlife

Shaba National Reserve is home to a diverse range of wildlife adapted to the semi-arid conditions. The reserve is known for its populations of elephants, lions, leopards, and cheetahs. Shaba is one of the best places to see the "Shaba Special Five," which includes the reticulated giraffe, Grevy's zebra, Somali ostrich, Beisa oryx, and gerenuk. These species are well adapted to the harsh environment and are less commonly found in other parts of Kenya. The Ewaso Ng'iro River supports a variety of aquatic species, including hippos and crocodiles. Birdwatchers will appreciate the reserve's rich avian diversity, with over 350 bird species, including the vibrant lilac-breasted roller and the African fish eagle.

Tourism activities

Tourism in Shaba National Reserve focuses on its unique wildlife and rugged landscapes. Game drives are the primary activity, offering visitors the opportunity to observe the reserve's diverse wildlife and enjoy its dramatic scenery. The riverbanks and floodplains provide excellent spots for wildlife viewing and photography. Birdwatching is popular, with numerous species to spot throughout the year. Cultural visits to nearby Samburu communities allow visitors to learn about the local Samburu people's traditions and lifestyle. Guided nature walks and night drives offer additional ways to explore the reserve and experience its natural beauty.

Conservation efforts

Conservation efforts in Shaba National Reserve are crucial for preserving its unique ecosystems and protecting its specialized wildlife. The reserve is managed by the Kenya Wildlife Service (KWS) in collaboration with local communities and conservation organizations. Key initiatives include anti-poaching measures, habitat management, and the protection of water sources such as the Ewaso Ng'iro River. Community-based conservation programs involve local communities in wildlife protection and sustainable land use practices. Research and monitoring activities help track wildlife populations and inform conservation strategies. Efforts to mitigate human-wildlife conflicts and promote sustainable tourism practices are integral to the reserve's conservation success.

Accessibility and accommodation

Shaba National Reserve is accessible by road and air. It is approximately a 5 to 6-hour drive from Nairobi, depending on road conditions and traffic. The reserve can also be reached by scheduled flights from Nairobi to the nearby airstrip, with flight times typically ranging from 1 hour to 1 hour 30 minutes. Accommodation options within and around the reserve include a range of lodges and tented camps, from mid-range to luxury. Notable lodges include the Sarova Shaba Game Lodge, which offers comfortable facilities and easy access to the reserve's attractions. Many accommodations offer game drives, guided walks, and other safari activities, providing a comprehensive wildlife experience.

Boni National Reserve

Introduction

Boni National Reserve, located in northeastern Kenya, is a pristine and remote wildlife sanctuary known for its lush rainforests and diverse ecosystems. Established in 1976, the reserve spans approximately 1,100 square kilometers and is situated in the coastal region of Lamu County. Boni National Reserve is renowned for its unique biodiversity, including several endemic and rare species, and offers a rich and unspoiled natural environment. The reserve is managed by the Kenya Wildlife Service (KWS) and provides important habitat for both wildlife and local communities.

Landscape and climate

The landscape of Boni National Reserve is characterized by its dense rainforests, rolling hills, and meandering rivers. The reserve features a variety of ecosystems, including tropical lowland forests, swampy areas, and open savannahs. The terrain is largely flat with some undulating hills, providing diverse habitats for wildlife. The climate is generally humid and tropical, with temperatures ranging from 20°C to 30°C (68°F to 86°F). Boni experiences two main rainy seasons: the long rains from March to May and the short rains from October to December. The high rainfall contributes to the lush vegetation and supports the reserve's rich biodiversity.

Wildlife

Boni National Reserve is home to a variety of wildlife species adapted to its tropical rainforest environment. The reserve supports populations of elephants, buffaloes, and various antelope species, including the bushbuck and the common duiker. Boni is notable for its rare and elusive primates, such as the endangered red colobus monkey and the Sykes' monkey. The reserve's diverse birdlife includes several endemic and migrant species, such as the Somali ostrich and the African grey parrot. The reserve's waterways and wetlands also support aquatic species, including crocodiles and hippos.

Tourism activities

Tourism in Boni National Reserve focuses on exploring its rich biodiversity and unique landscapes. Wildlife viewing is the primary activity, with opportunities to observe the reserve's diverse species in their natural habitat. Birdwatching is popular, given the reserve's extensive avian diversity. The dense rainforests and wetlands offer excellent opportunities for nature photography and exploration. Cultural visits to nearby local communities provide insights into the traditions and lifestyles of the coastal populations. Guided nature walks and hikes are available, allowing visitors to experience the reserve's natural beauty up close.

Conservation efforts

Conservation efforts in Boni National Reserve aim to protect its unique ecosystems and safeguard its diverse wildlife. The reserve is managed by the Kenya Wildlife Service in collaboration with local communities and conservation organizations. Key conservation initiatives include anti-poaching measures, habitat preservation, and the protection of key species such as the red colobus monkey. Community-based conservation programs involve local residents in wildlife protection and sustainable land use practices. Research and monitoring activities help track wildlife populations and inform conservation strategies. Efforts to address human-wildlife conflicts and promote eco-friendly tourism practices are integral to the reserve's conservation success.

Accessibility and accommodation

Boni National Reserve is accessible by road and air. The reserve is approximately a 6 to 7-hour drive from Nairobi, depending on road conditions and traffic. The nearest major town is Lamu, which is connected to Nairobi by scheduled flights. From Lamu, visitors can travel by road or boat to reach the reserve. Accommodation options within and around the reserve are limited and include a few eco-lodges and campsites that offer basic amenities. Visitors may need to make arrangements in advance and consider staying in nearby Lamu or Garsen for additional options. Many accommodations offer guided tours, wildlife viewing, and cultural experiences.

Arawale National Reserve

Introduction

Arawale National Reserve is a lesser-known wildlife sanctuary located in northeastern Kenya, in Garissa County. Covering approximately 533 square kilometers, this reserve was established in 1974 with the primary goal of protecting the critically endangered hirola antelope, also known as the Hunter's antelope. Arawale is one of Kenya's most important conservation areas due to its efforts to protect this rare species, as well as its role in preserving the unique ecosystems of the Tana River region. The reserve remains relatively undisturbed, offering a glimpse into Kenya's more remote and untouched natural habitats.

Landscape and climate

The landscape of Arawale National Reserve is characterized by its semi-arid environment, featuring open savannahs, scrublands, and acacia woodlands. The reserve is located near the Tana River, which provides a vital water source and supports a variety of riparian vegetation along its banks. The terrain is generally flat, with scattered bushlands and occasional rocky outcrops. The climate in Arawale is hot and dry, with temperatures typically ranging from 25°C to 35°C (77°F to 95°F). The area experiences two main rainy seasons: the long rains from March to May and the short rains from October to December, though rainfall is generally sparse.

Wildlife

Arawale National Reserve is most famous for being one of the last strongholds of the hirola antelope, one of the world's rarest and most endangered antelope species. The reserve is a critical habitat for this species, which is endemic to the border region of Kenya and Somalia. Besides the hirola, Arawale is home to other wildlife species such as elephants, giraffes, zebras, and various antelopes, including Grant's gazelle and the lesser kudu. Predators such as lions, cheetahs, and hyenas also roam the reserve. Birdlife is diverse, with several species adapted to the arid conditions, including the Somali ostrich and various raptors.

Tourism activities

Tourism in Arawale National Reserve is limited due to its remote location and the challenges associated with accessing the area. However, for the adventurous traveler, the reserve offers unique wildlife viewing opportunities, particularly for those interested in seeing the rare hirola antelope. Game drives and nature walks are the primary activities, allowing visitors to explore the reserve's diverse habitats and observe its wildlife. The Tana River, which flows near the reserve, offers additional opportunities for birdwatching and exploring riparian ecosystems. Due to its undisturbed nature, Arawale also provides excellent opportunities for photography, particularly for those interested in documenting rare species and remote landscapes.

Conservation efforts

Conservation efforts in Arawale National Reserve are focused primarily on the protection of the hirola antelope, which has seen a dramatic decline in numbers due to habitat loss, hunting, and competition with livestock. The reserve was established specifically to create a safe haven for this species, and ongoing efforts include habitat restoration, anti-poaching measures, and community-based conservation programs. The Kenya Wildlife Service (KWS) works closely with local communities to promote sustainable land use practices and to reduce human-wildlife conflicts. Research and monitoring programs are also in place to track the population of the hirola and other key species, informing conservation strategies aimed at preventing further decline.

Accessibility and accommodation

Arawale National Reserve is located in a remote area of northeastern Kenya, making accessibility challenging. The reserve is approximately 240 kilometers from Garissa town, the nearest major center, and the journey can take several hours by road, depending on conditions. There are no direct flights to the reserve, so visitors must travel by road, often requiring a 4x4 vehicle due to the rough terrain.

Accommodation options within the reserve are very limited, with basic camping facilities being the primary option for those who wish to stay overnight. Visitors may also find accommodation in nearby towns like Garissa or choose to stay in mobile camps set up specifically for expeditions into the reserve.

Bisanadi National Reserve

Introduction

Bisanadi National Reserve is a remote and rugged wildlife reserve located in eastern Kenya, near the border with Meru National Park. Established in 1979, the reserve covers approximately 606 square kilometers and serves as a crucial buffer zone between the more popular Meru National Park and the expansive wilderness of the northern frontier. Bisanadi is part of the larger Meru Conservation Area, which includes Meru, Kora, and Mwingi National Reserves. The reserve is managed by the Kenya Wildlife Service (KWS) and offers a truly wild and unspoiled safari experience, with limited human interference and vast, untamed landscapes.

Landscape and climate

The landscape of Bisanadi National Reserve is characterized by its semi-arid terrain, featuring open savannahs, dense bushlands, and scattered riverine forests along the banks of the Tana and Bisanadi Rivers. The reserve's terrain is largely flat, with occasional rocky outcrops and seasonal floodplains that support a variety of vegetation types. The climate is generally hot and dry, with temperatures ranging from 25°C to 35°C (77°F to 95°F). Bisanadi experiences two main rainy seasons: the long rains from March to May and the short rains from October to December, although the region receives less rainfall compared to the neighboring Meru National Park, contributing to its more arid conditions.

Wildlife

Bisanadi National Reserve is home to a variety of wildlife species, many of which migrate between the reserve and the adjacent Meru National Park. The reserve supports populations of elephants, lions, leopards, and buffaloes, as well as a range of herbivores such as giraffes, zebras, and various antelope species including the lesser kudu, eland, and oryx. The Tana and Bisanadi Rivers are crucial lifelines for the reserve's wildlife, providing water sources during the dry seasons. The rivers also support aquatic species such as hippos and crocodiles. Birdlife in Bisanadi is diverse, with species adapted to the semi-arid environment, including raptors, waterfowl, and numerous smaller birds.

Tourism activities

Tourism in Bisanadi National Reserve is limited, making it an ideal destination for those seeking solitude and a more authentic wilderness experience. The reserve's remote location and rugged terrain offer excellent opportunities for game viewing, particularly for those interested in exploring less-crowded areas. Game drives are the primary activity, allowing visitors to observe the reserve's diverse wildlife in its natural habitat. The riverside areas provide good opportunities for birdwatching and wildlife photography. The reserve's unspoiled environment also offers opportunities for guided nature walks, although these are typically arranged through nearby Meru National Park due to the lack of facilities within Bisanadi itself.

Conservation efforts

Conservation efforts in Bisanadi National Reserve focus on maintaining its role as a vital buffer zone and migration corridor between Meru National Park and the northern wilderness areas. The reserve is managed by the Kenya Wildlife Service, which works to protect its wildlife and habitats from threats such as poaching and habitat degradation. Anti-poaching patrols, habitat restoration, and community engagement are key components of the reserve's conservation strategy. Bisanadi's inclusion in the larger Meru

Conservation Area helps to ensure that wildlife can move freely between protected areas, maintaining healthy populations and genetic diversity. Collaboration with local communities is also important in promoting sustainable land use practices and reducing human-wildlife conflicts.

Accessibility and accommodation

Bisanadi National Reserve is remote and challenging to access, which contributes to its appeal for those seeking a true wilderness experience. The reserve is located near Meru National Park, and the closest major town is Meru, which is about a 5 to 6-hour drive from Nairobi. Visitors typically access Bisanadi via Meru National Park, traveling through rugged terrain that often requires a 4x4 vehicle. There are no formal accommodation facilities within Bisanadi National Reserve itself, but visitors can stay in lodges, camps, or guesthouses in Meru National Park or the nearby towns. Some of these accommodations offer guided tours and game drives that can include visits to Bisanadi.

Kora National Reserve

Introduction

Kora National Reserve is a rugged and remote wildlife reserve located in eastern Kenya, covering an area of approximately 1,787 square kilometers. Established in 1973, Kora is often referred to as the "Last Wilderness" due to its vast, untamed landscapes and low levels of human habitation. The reserve gained international fame through the efforts of conservationist George Adamson, who worked here to rehabilitate and release lions back into the wild. Kora is part of the larger Meru Conservation Area, which includes Meru National Park and other adjacent reserves. The reserve is managed by the Kenya Wildlife Service (KWS) and remains a key site for wildlife conservation and biodiversity.

Landscape and climate

The landscape of Kora National Reserve is characterized by its dramatic and diverse terrain, which includes rocky hills, granite outcrops, dry riverbeds, and expansive plains. The Tana River, one of Kenya's major rivers, forms the northern boundary of the reserve and is a vital water source for the wildlife. The reserve's landscape is dotted with baobab trees, acacia woodlands, and patches of dense bushland. Kora's climate is generally hot and arid, with temperatures often exceeding 30°C (86°F) during the day. The area experiences two main rainy seasons: the long rains from March to May and the short rains from October to December, though rainfall is generally low, contributing to the semi-arid conditions.

Wildlife

Kora National Reserve is home to a diverse array of wildlife, including several species that are well-adapted to its harsh environment. The reserve supports populations of large mammals such as elephants, lions, leopards, cheetahs, and hyenas. Kora is also known for its significant populations of herbivores, including giraffes, zebras, and various antelope species such as the lesser kudu, oryx, and eland. The Tana River is a key feature of the reserve, attracting hippos and crocodiles, as well as a variety of bird species, particularly waterfowl. The reserve's rugged terrain and remote location make it an ideal habitat for some of Kenya's more elusive wildlife, including the caracal and serval.

Tourism activities

Tourism in Kora National Reserve is limited, making it an ideal destination for those seeking a truly wild and secluded safari experience. The reserve's remote location and rugged terrain offer excellent opportunities for game viewing, particularly for those interested in exploring less-visited areas. Game drives are the primary activity, allowing visitors to traverse the vast landscapes and observe the reserve's diverse wildlife. Birdwatching is also a popular activity, given the reserve's diverse avian population. The Tana River offers opportunities for fishing and exploring the riverine forests. Kora's historical significance, as the former home of George Adamson, adds an element of cultural and conservation history to the visit.

Conservation efforts

Conservation efforts in Kora National Reserve are focused on preserving its unique ecosystems and protecting its wildlife from threats such as poaching and habitat loss. The reserve was originally established as a refuge for wildlife, particularly for big cats like lions, and these conservation goals remain central to its management. The Kenya Wildlife Service (KWS) conducts regular anti-poaching patrols and works to maintain the integrity of the reserve's habitats. The reserve's connection to George Adamson's work has also inspired ongoing efforts to protect big cats and other large mammals. Community involvement in conservation is promoted through education and sustainable land use practices, helping to reduce human-wildlife conflicts and ensure the long-term survival of the reserve's wildlife.

Accessibility and accommodation

Kora National Reserve is remote and challenging to access, which contributes to its appeal for those seeking a more isolated wilderness experience. The reserve is located about 280 kilometers northeast of Nairobi, and the journey by road can take several hours, often requiring a 4x4 vehicle due to the rough terrain. The nearest airstrip is in Meru National Park, from where visitors can drive to Kora. Accommodation options within the reserve are limited, with only basic campsites available for those who wish to stay overnight. These campsites offer a truly immersive experience, allowing visitors to camp under the stars in the heart of the wilderness. Additional accommodation options, including lodges and camps, can be found in the nearby Meru National Park, which offers more amenities and organized tours.

Mwingi National Reserve

Introduction

Mwingi National Reserve is a remote and expansive wildlife sanctuary located in eastern Kenya, adjacent to Kora National Reserve and part of the larger Meru Conservation Area. Covering an area of approximately 745 square kilometers, Mwingi is one of Kenya's lesser-known reserves, offering a pristine and undisturbed wilderness experience. The reserve was established to protect its unique biodiversity, including various endangered species, and to serve as a buffer zone between Kora National Reserve and the surrounding human settlements. Mwingi National Reserve is managed by the Kenya Wildlife Service (KWS) and remains a hidden gem for those seeking solitude and adventure in Kenya's wild landscapes.

Landscape and climate

Mwingi National Reserve is characterized by its rugged and varied terrain, which includes rolling hills, rocky outcrops, dry riverbeds, and expansive plains. The reserve is largely semi-arid, with vegetation ranging from acacia woodlands and bushlands to open savannahs and scattered patches of riverine forest along seasonal rivers such as the Tana and Ura Rivers. The climate in Mwingi is hot and dry, with temperatures often exceeding 30°C (86°F) during the day. The reserve experiences two main rainy seasons: the long rains from March to May and the short rains from October to December. However, rainfall is generally low, contributing to the reserve's semi-arid conditions.

Wildlife

Mwingi National Reserve is home to a diverse array of wildlife, much of which migrates between the reserve and the adjacent Kora and Meru National Reserves. Large mammals such as elephants, lions, leopards, and cheetahs are present in the reserve, alongside herbivores like giraffes, zebras, and various antelope species, including the lesser kudu, oryx, and eland. The Tana and Ura Rivers are critical water sources for the reserve's wildlife, especially during the dry seasons. These rivers also support aquatic species such as hippos and crocodiles. Birdlife in Mwingi is rich, with species adapted to the arid environment, including raptors, waterfowl, and numerous smaller birds.

Tourism activities

Tourism in Mwingi National Reserve is limited, making it an ideal destination for those seeking an off-the-beaten-path experience in Kenya's wilderness. The reserve's remote location and rugged terrain offer excellent opportunities for game viewing, particularly for those interested in exploring areas that are less frequented by tourists. Game drives are the primary activity, allowing visitors to traverse the vast landscapes and observe the diverse wildlife. Birdwatching is also popular, with the reserve's varied habitats supporting a wide range of bird species. The Tana River offers opportunities for fishing and exploring the riverine ecosystems. Due to the reserve's relative isolation, visitors can enjoy a quiet and intimate safari experience, far from the crowds of more popular parks.

Conservation efforts

Conservation efforts in Mwingi National Reserve focus on protecting its unique ecosystems and the wildlife that inhabits them. The reserve plays a crucial role as a buffer zone between Kora National Reserve and human settlements, helping to reduce human-wildlife conflicts and preserve the integrity of the larger Meru Conservation Area. The Kenya Wildlife Service (KWS) is responsible for managing the reserve and implementing conservation strategies, including anti-poaching patrols, habitat restoration, and community engagement programs. These efforts aim to protect endangered species, such as the hirola antelope and the Grevy's zebra, which are found within the reserve, as well as to promote sustainable land use practices among local communities.

Accessibility and accommodation

Mwingi National Reserve is remote and not easily accessible, which adds to its appeal for those seeking a truly wild and secluded safari experience. The reserve is located approximately 300 kilometers northeast of Nairobi, and the journey by road can take several hours, often requiring a 4x4 vehicle due to the rough terrain. The nearest airstrip is in Meru National Park, from where visitors can drive to Mwingi. Accommodation options within the reserve are limited, with only basic campsites available for those who wish to stay overnight. These campsites provide an authentic wilderness experience, allowing visitors to camp under the stars and immerse themselves in the natural surroundings. Additional accommodation options, including lodges and camps, can be found in the nearby Meru National Park, which offers more amenities and organized tours.

Kakamega Forest National Reserve

Introduction

Kakamega Forest National Reserve is a unique and biodiverse rainforest located in western Kenya. Covering approximately 238 square kilometers, this reserve is the last remnant of the ancient Guineo-Congolian rainforest that once stretched across Central Africa. The forest is renowned for its rich biodiversity, including numerous endemic species of flora and fauna that cannot be found elsewhere in Kenya. Kakamega Forest is not only a vital conservation area but also a significant cultural and ecological site, often referred to as Kenya's only tropical rainforest.

Landscape and climate

Kakamega Forest National Reserve is characterized by its dense, tropical rainforest landscape, featuring towering trees, lush undergrowth, and a network of rivers and streams that nourish the ecosystem. The forest is interspersed with clearings, swamps, and patches of bamboo groves, creating a varied and complex environment. The terrain is gently undulating, with elevations ranging from 1,500 to 1,700 meters above sea level. Kakamega's climate is warm and humid, with temperatures averaging between 20°C and 30°C (68°F to 86°F) year-round. The reserve receives substantial rainfall, particularly during the long rainy season from March to May and the short rains from

October to December. This high level of precipitation supports the lush vegetation and the rich biodiversity within the forest.

Wildlife

Kakamega Forest National Reserve is a biodiversity hotspot, home to a wide variety of species, many of which are unique to the region. The forest is particularly famous for its birdlife, with over 360 species recorded, including the rare Great Blue Turaco, Turner's Eremomela, and the Blue-headed Bee-eater. Mammals such as black-and-white colobus monkeys, De Brazza's monkeys, and potto (a type of nocturnal primate) inhabit the forest, along with a range of small mammals like duikers, squirrels, and bushbucks. The reserve is also home to numerous amphibians, reptiles, and invertebrates, including a diverse array of butterflies, some of which are endemic to the forest. The dense canopy and complex ecosystem make Kakamega an important sanctuary for these species, many of which are not found in other parts of Kenya.

Tourism activities

Kakamega Forest National Reserve offers a variety of activities for nature enthusiasts and visitors looking to experience Kenya's only tropical rainforest. Birdwatching is one of the most popular activities, given the reserve's rich avian diversity. Guided nature walks are available, allowing visitors to explore the forest's trails, discover its unique flora, and observe wildlife in their natural habitats. These walks often include visits to key sites such as the Isiukhu Falls, the Yala River, and ancient trees that are over 300 years old. The reserve's serene environment is also ideal for meditation, picnicking, and photography, with opportunities to capture the forest's vibrant colors and wildlife. For those interested in cultural experiences, the reserve is close to local communities, where visitors can learn about the traditions and lifestyles of the Luhya people, who have lived in harmony with the forest for generations.

Conservation efforts

Conservation efforts in Kakamega Forest National Reserve are critical to preserving its unique ecosystem and biodiversity. The reserve faces several threats, including illegal logging, encroachment, and agricultural expansion. To address these challenges, the Kenya Wildlife Service (KWS), in collaboration with local and international conservation organizations, has implemented various strategies aimed at protecting the forest. These include strict anti-poaching measures, reforestation programs, and community-based conservation initiatives. One of the key aspects of these efforts is involving local communities in sustainable land-use practices and providing them with alternative livelihoods to reduce dependence on forest resources. Education and awareness programs are also conducted to emphasize the importance of conservation and the role of the forest in maintaining ecological balance in the region.

Accessibility and accommodation

Kakamega Forest National Reserve is relatively accessible, located about 50 kilometers north of Kisumu and 418 kilometers northwest of Nairobi. The reserve can be reached by road from Kisumu or Kakamega town, with the journey taking approximately one hour from either location. The nearest airstrip is in Kisumu, which is served by daily flights from Nairobi. Within the reserve, several accommodation options cater to different preferences and budgets. These include eco-lodges, guesthouses, and campsites, all of which offer comfortable stays and opportunities to experience the forest's tranquility. Popular accommodations include the Rondo Retreat Center, which provides rustic charm and access to the forest trails, and Udo's Bandas, offering more basic facilities for budget travelers. Camping is also an option for those who wish to immerse themselves fully in the forest environment.

Rahole National Reserve

Introduction

Rahole National Reserve is a vast and remote protected area located in northeastern Kenya, near the Tana River and close to the border with Somalia. Covering approximately 1,250 square kilometers, Rahole is part of a larger network of reserves and parks in the region, including the adjacent Kora and Mwingi National Reserves. Established to protect the unique ecosystems and wildlife of this arid region, Rahole is one of Kenya's lesser-known reserves, offering a pristine wilderness experience for those seeking solitude and adventure. The reserve is managed by the Kenya Wildlife Service (KWS) and remains an important conservation area for the diverse flora and fauna that inhabit this harsh environment.

Landscape and climate

Rahole National Reserve is characterized by its arid and semi-arid landscape, which includes open savannahs, scrublands, and scattered patches of acacia woodlands. The terrain is generally flat, with some rocky outcrops and seasonal rivers that flow through the reserve, providing critical water sources for wildlife. The Tana River, located to the west of the reserve, plays a vital role in sustaining the ecosystems of the region, particularly during the dry seasons. Rahole's climate is hot and dry, with temperatures often exceeding 30°C (86°F) during the day. The area receives minimal rainfall, primarily during the long rains from March to May and the short rains from October to December. The harsh climate and arid conditions have shaped the reserve's unique landscape and the species that have adapted to survive there.

Wildlife

Rahole National Reserve is home to a variety of wildlife species that have adapted to the arid environment. Large mammals such as elephants, lions, leopards, and cheetahs are present in the reserve, although they are more elusive due to the vast and sparsely populated landscape. The reserve also supports populations of herbivores, including giraffes, zebras, and various antelope species such as the gerenuk, lesser kudu, and oryx. The Tana River and other seasonal water sources attract hippos and crocodiles, as well as a range of bird species, making the reserve a potential birdwatching destination. Rahole's remote location and low levels of human activity provide a safe haven for these species, many of which migrate between Rahole and the surrounding reserves and parks.

Tourism activities

Tourism in Rahole National Reserve is minimal, making it an ideal destination for those seeking an off-the-beaten-path safari experience. The reserve's vast, open landscapes offer excellent opportunities for game viewing, particularly for visitors interested in exploring less commercialized and more rugged areas. Game drives are the primary activity, allowing visitors to traverse the reserve and observe its wildlife in their natural habitats. Given the reserve's remote location, tourists can enjoy a quiet and undisturbed experience, far from the crowds that frequent Kenya's more popular parks. Birdwatching is another potential activity, especially around the Tana River, where a variety of waterfowl and other bird species can be observed. However, due to the reserve's isolation and limited infrastructure, tourism activities are largely self-guided, catering to more adventurous and experienced travelers.

Conservation efforts

Conservation efforts in Rahole National Reserve focus on preserving its unique ecosystems and protecting the wildlife that inhabit them. The reserve's remote location has helped shield it from some of the pressures faced by other protected areas, such as poaching and habitat encroachment. However, the region's arid conditions and the challenges of managing such a vast and sparsely populated area make Conservation efforts essential. The Kenya Wildlife Service (KWS) is responsible for overseeing the reserve and implementing conservation strategies, including anti-poaching patrols and habitat monitoring. Collaboration with local communities is also crucial, as these communities often depend on the land for their livelihoods.

Education and awareness programs are conducted to promote sustainable land use practices and reduce human-wildlife conflicts, ensuring the long-term survival of the reserve's ecosystems.

Accessibility and accommodation

Rahole National Reserve is one of Kenya's more remote and less accessible reserves, located far from major cities and towns. The reserve is approximately 350 kilometers northeast of Nairobi, and reaching it by road can be challenging due to the rough terrain and the need for a 4x4 vehicle. The nearest airstrip is in Garissa, which is around 200 kilometers away, from where visitors can drive to the reserve. Given its remote location, Rahole has very limited accommodation options. There are no established lodges or camps within the reserve itself, so visitors typically need to be self-sufficient, bringing their own camping equipment and supplies. Camping in the reserve offers a unique opportunity to experience the wilderness up close, but it requires careful planning and preparation. Nearby towns such as Garissa or Mwingi may offer basic accommodation options for those who prefer not to camp in the reserve.

Manda National Reserve

Introduction

Manda National Reserve is a little-known protected area located on the eastern shores of Lake Turkana in northern Kenya. This reserve is part of the greater Turkana Basin, an area renowned for its archaeological significance and unique ecosystems. Covering an area of approximately 1,500 square kilometers, Manda National Reserve is a vital sanctuary for wildlife that has adapted to the harsh, arid environment surrounding Lake Turkana. Despite its remote location and challenging conditions, the reserve plays a critical role in the conservation of the region's biodiversity and offers a unique experience for the intrepid traveler.

Landscape and climate

Manda National Reserve is characterized by its stark, rugged terrain, dominated by arid landscapes, volcanic outcrops, and the expansive shores of Lake Turkana. The reserve's landscape is primarily semi-desert, with sparse vegetation comprising acacia woodlands, thorny bushes, and scattered scrubland. The proximity to Lake Turkana, the world's largest desert lake, adds to the reserve's unique environment, with the lake's turquoise waters contrasting sharply against the barren land. The climate in Manda National Reserve is hot and dry, with temperatures frequently soaring above 30°C (86°F) and minimal rainfall throughout the year. The long dry spells are punctuated by brief rainy seasons, typically from March to May and October to December, although rainfall is often irregular and insufficient.

Wildlife

Despite the harsh conditions, Manda National Reserve supports a variety of wildlife species that have adapted to the arid environment. Large mammals such as elephants, lions, and leopards are known to inhabit the reserve, although they are less commonly sighted due to the challenging terrain and vast expanses of the area. The reserve is also home to smaller mammals, including hyenas, jackals, and various antelope species such as the Grant's gazelle, Grevy's zebra, and oryx. Reptiles, particularly crocodiles, are found along the shores of Lake Turkana, and the lake itself is home to a significant population of Nile tilapia and other fish species. Birdlife in the reserve is diverse, with both resident and migratory species present, including flamingos, pelicans, and a variety of raptors. The unique ecosystem of Manda National Reserve, shaped by its proximity to Lake Turkana, makes it an important refuge for wildlife in this arid region.

Tourism activities

Tourism in Manda National Reserve is minimal due to its remote location and the challenging conditions. However, for adventurous travelers and those with a deep interest in natural history and archaeology, the reserve offers a truly unique experience. Visitors can explore the rugged landscapes, observe the hardy wildlife, and enjoy the breathtaking views of Lake Turkana. Game drives are the primary activity, allowing tourists to traverse the reserve's vast terrain and potentially spot the wildlife that roams this remote area. Birdwatching is also popular, especially along the lake's shores where a variety of waterbirds can be seen. The reserve's proximity to Lake Turkana makes it an excellent base for exploring the lake's islands and the nearby archaeological sites, which are part of the world-renowned Turkana Basin. Due to the reserve's remote nature, tourism activities are often self-guided or arranged through specialized tour operators who are familiar with the area.

Conservation efforts

Conservation in Manda National Reserve is essential to preserving its unique ecosystems and the wildlife that depends on them. The reserve faces several challenges, including the harsh climate, limited resources, and the potential impacts of climate change on Lake Turkana's water levels and the surrounding environment. The Kenya Wildlife Service (KWS) oversees the management of the reserve, focusing on protecting its natural habitats, preventing poaching, and mitigating human-wildlife conflicts. Given the reserve's remote location, community involvement in Conservation efforts is crucial. Local communities are encouraged to participate in sustainable land use practices and conservation initiatives, which help to protect the reserve's biodiversity while supporting the livelihoods of the people who live in the region.

Accessibility and accommodation

Manda National Reserve is one of Kenya's more remote and challenging reserves to access. The reserve is located in the northern part of the country, near the eastern shores of Lake Turkana. Reaching the reserve typically involves a long journey by road from Nairobi or other major towns, often requiring a 4x4 vehicle due to the rough and rugged terrain. The nearest airstrips are in Lodwar and Kalokol, both of which are several hours' drive from the reserve. Accommodation within the reserve is extremely limited, with few established facilities available. Visitors typically need to be self-sufficient, bringing their own camping equipment and supplies. The nearby town of Lodwar offers basic accommodation options for those who prefer not to camp. Despite the challenges of accessibility, the reserve's isolation and rugged beauty make it an attractive destination for those seeking to explore one of Kenya's most untouched wilderness areas.

Dodori National Reserve

Introduction

Dodori National Reserve is a remote and ecologically significant protected area located in the Lamu County of northeastern Kenya, near the border with Somalia. Established in 1976, the reserve covers approximately 877 square kilometers and is part of the larger Lamu Archipelago conservation complex, which also includes the Boni National Reserve. Dodori is named after the Dodori River, which flows through the reserve and into the Indian Ocean. This reserve is notable for its diverse ecosystems, which range from coastal mangrove forests to inland woodlands and savannahs, and is a critical habitat for several endangered and rare species. Dodori National Reserve remains one of Kenya's lesser-known wildlife sanctuaries, offering a pristine environment for wildlife conservation and a unique experience for intrepid travelers.

Landscape and climate

Dodori National Reserve features a diverse landscape that includes coastal plains, riverine forests, mangroves, and savannahs. The reserve is situated along the Indian Ocean, with the Dodori River playing a central role in the ecosystem, particularly in maintaining the lush riverine forests that thrive along its banks. The mangrove forests are among the most extensive in Kenya, providing crucial breeding grounds for marine life and serving as a buffer against coastal erosion. Inland, the terrain transitions into open grasslands and wooded areas, creating a varied environment that supports a wide range of species. The climate in Dodori is typically hot and humid, with temperatures averaging between 25°C and 35°C (77°F to 95°F). The area experiences two main rainy seasons: the long rains from March to May and the short rains from October to December, which are vital for replenishing the reserve's water sources and supporting its diverse habitats.

Wildlife

Dodori National Reserve is home to a rich array of wildlife, many of which are adapted to the unique coastal and savannah ecosystems. The reserve is a haven for large mammals such as elephants, buffaloes, and the endangered hirola antelope, also known as the Hunter's hartebeest, which is one of the world's rarest antelope species. The reserve's coastal location makes it an important breeding ground for marine species, including sea turtles, which nest on the reserve's beaches. The mangrove and riverine forests provide shelter for a variety of bird species, making Dodori a potential birdwatching destination. Among the notable bird species are the African fish eagle, palm-nut vulture, and various wading birds. The reserve also supports populations of carnivores, including lions, leopards, and hyenas, although these are less frequently seen due to the dense vegetation and vast expanses of the area.

Tourism activities

Dodori National Reserve is a remote and rarely visited area, making it an ideal destination for those seeking solitude and a true wilderness experience. The reserve's pristine landscapes and diverse ecosystems offer opportunities for game viewing, where visitors can explore the reserve's savannahs and riverine forests to observe its wildlife in their natural habitats. Birdwatching is another popular activity, particularly along the Dodori River and the mangrove forests, where a variety of bird species can be spotted. The coastal location of the reserve also offers opportunities for marine activities, such as turtle watching during the nesting season and exploring the mangrove ecosystems. Due to its remote location, tourism in Dodori is primarily for the adventurous traveler, and activities are often self-guided or arranged through specialized tour operators familiar with the area.

Conservation efforts

Dodori National Reserve plays a crucial role in the conservation of several endangered and vulnerable species, particularly the hirola antelope and marine turtles. The reserve is managed by the Kenya Wildlife Service (KWS) in collaboration with local and international conservation organizations. Conservation efforts focus on protecting the reserve's diverse habitats from threats such as poaching, illegal logging, and habitat destruction. Anti-poaching patrols are regularly conducted to safeguard the wildlife, and community engagement is key to conservation success in the region. Local communities are encouraged to participate in sustainable land-use practices and to take part in conservation activities, such as monitoring turtle nests and protecting critical breeding grounds. Education and awareness campaigns are also conducted to promote the importance of preserving the unique ecosystems within the reserve.

Accessibility and accommodation

Dodori National Reserve is one of Kenya's more remote and difficult-to-access reserves. It is located in the northeastern part of the country, near the town of Kiunga, which serves as the gateway to the reserve. The reserve is approximately 500 kilometers from Nairobi, and reaching it by road requires a long and challenging journey, often necessitating the use of a 4x4 vehicle. The nearest airstrip is in Lamu, from where visitors can travel by road or boat to the reserve. Due to its isolation, there are very few accommodation options within or near the reserve. Visitors typically need to be self-sufficient, bringing their own camping gear and supplies. There are limited facilities for camping, and any visits to the reserve should be well-planned in advance, ideally with the assistance of experienced tour operators. For those seeking more comfort, basic lodges and guesthouses are available in Lamu or Kiunga, where visitors can stay before embarking on a journey into the reserve.

Ndere Island National Park

Introduction

Ndere Island National Park is a picturesque and serene protected area located in Lake Victoria, Kenya's largest freshwater lake. Established in 1986, the park covers approximately 4.2 square kilometers and is situated in Siaya County, just off the northern shore of Lake Victoria. The name "Ndere" means "meeting place" in the local Luo language, highlighting the island's cultural significance to the surrounding communities. Ndere Island is often referred to as the "Jewel of Lake Victoria" due to its unspoiled natural beauty, lush vegetation, and tranquil environment. The park is an ideal destination for nature lovers, birdwatchers, and those seeking a peaceful retreat away from the bustling mainland.

Landscape and climate

Ndere Island National Park features a diverse landscape characterized by rolling hills, grassy plains, and thick forests. The island's terrain gently rises from the shores of Lake Victoria, providing stunning panoramic views of the surrounding waters and mainland. The vegetation on the island is primarily composed of acacia woodlands, tall grasses, and patches of indigenous forest, which support a variety of wildlife. The park's location within Lake Victoria ensures a moderate tropical climate, with temperatures ranging from 20°C to 30°C (68°F to 86°F) throughout the year. The region experiences two main rainy seasons: the long rains from March to May and the short rains from October to December, which help sustain the island's lush vegetation and water sources.

Wildlife

Despite its small size, Ndere Island National Park is home to a variety of wildlife species, many of which have adapted to the island's unique ecosystem. The park is a sanctuary for the rare and endangered sitatunga antelope, which thrives in the island's wetlands and marshy areas. Other herbivores found on the island include impalas, warthogs, and zebras, which graze on the open grasslands. The park is also a haven for birdlife, with over 100 recorded species, making it a popular destination for birdwatchers. Notable bird species include the African fish eagle, black-headed gonolek, and the magnificent grey-crowned crane. The surrounding waters of Lake Victoria are rich in fish, including the Nile perch and tilapia, attracting a variety of aquatic birds and providing sustenance for the island's wildlife.

Tourism activities

Ndere Island National Park offers a range of activities for visitors to enjoy, making it an attractive destination for eco-tourists and nature enthusiasts. The island's serene environment is perfect for nature walks and hiking, with trails that wind through the diverse landscapes, offering opportunities to spot wildlife and enjoy scenic views of Lake Victoria. Birdwatching is a major draw, with the island's varied habitats providing ideal conditions for observing a wide range of bird species. Picnicking is another popular activity, with designated areas offering picturesque spots to relax and take in the natural beauty of the island. Boating and fishing can be arranged on Lake Victoria, allowing visitors to explore the waters around the island and try their hand at catching some of the lake's abundant fish. The island's peaceful atmosphere makes it a great location for meditation and photography, capturing the stunning landscapes and diverse wildlife.

Conservation efforts

Ndere Island National Park plays a crucial role in the conservation of its unique ecosystems and the species that inhabit them. Managed by the Kenya Wildlife Service (KWS), the park is protected from human encroachment and activities that could harm its natural environment. Conservation efforts focus on preserving the island's habitats, particularly the wetlands and forests that support the sitatunga antelope and the rich birdlife. Anti-poaching measures are in place to safeguard the wildlife, and regular monitoring of the park's ecosystems helps ensure that the natural balance is maintained. The park also engages with local communities to promote conservation awareness and sustainable tourism practices, ensuring that the benefits of the park are shared while minimizing negative impacts on the environment.

Accessibility and accommodation

Ndere Island National Park is accessible from the mainland by boat, with the nearest departure point being the town of Kisumu, located approximately 45 kilometers away. Visitors can reach Kisumu by road from Nairobi, a journey of about 5-6 hours, or by air, with regular flights available from Nairobi to Kisumu International Airport. From Kisumu, visitors can take a boat ride across Lake Victoria to Ndere Island, a journey that takes about 30-45 minutes. Once on the island, visitors can explore the park on foot, as the small size of the island makes it easy to navigate. Accommodation options near Ndere Island are limited, but there are several lodges, hotels, and guesthouses in Kisumu and the surrounding areas that cater to visitors. Camping is allowed on the island for those who wish to experience the park's natural beauty overnight, although visitors must bring their own camping gear and supplies.

Animal sanctuaries in Kenya

David Sheldrick Wildlife Trust (Elephant Orphanage)

Introduction

The David Sheldrick Wildlife Trust (DSWT), also known as the Elephant Orphanage, is a renowned wildlife conservation organization located in Nairobi, Kenya. Established in 1977 by Dr. Dame Daphne Sheldrick in memory of her late husband, David Sheldrick, a pioneering figure in wildlife conservation, the Trust is dedicated to the protection and preservation of Kenya's wildlife, particularly elephants. The Elephant Orphanage is the Trust's most famous initiative, providing a sanctuary for orphaned elephants and rhinos, many of whom have lost their families due to poaching or human-wildlife conflict. The Trust is not only a refuge for these animals but also a center for education and awareness, attracting thousands of visitors from around the world who come to learn about wildlife conservation and witness the rehabilitation of these majestic creatures.

Landscape and climate

The David Sheldrick Wildlife Trust is located within the Nairobi National Park, a unique urban wildlife reserve situated on the outskirts of Nairobi, Kenya's capital city. The park's landscape is a blend of open grasslands, acacia woodlands, and riverine forests, providing an ideal environment for the elephants and other animals at the orphanage. The climate in Nairobi is generally mild, with temperatures ranging from 10°C to 26°C (50°F to 79°F) throughout the year. The area experiences two main rainy seasons: the long rains from March to May and the short rains from October to December. The relatively stable climate allows for the year-round operation of the orphanage and ensures that the animals have access to natural vegetation and water sources.

Wildlife

The primary focus of the David Sheldrick Wildlife Trust is the care and rehabilitation of orphaned elephants and rhinos. These young animals, often traumatized by the loss of their families, receive round-the-clock care from dedicated keepers who act as surrogate parents. The orphanage provides a safe haven where the elephants are bottle-fed, nurtured, and socialized with other orphans in preparation for their eventual reintegration into the wild. In addition to elephants and rhinos, the Trust also cares for a variety of other wildlife species that may need assistance, including giraffes, zebras, and antelopes. The orphanage is also home to a diverse array of bird species, which thrive in the protected environment of Nairobi National Park.

Tourism activities

Visiting the David Sheldrick Wildlife Trust offers a unique and moving experience for wildlife enthusiasts and conservation supporters. The Elephant Orphanage is open to the public for a limited time each day, usually between 11:00 AM and 12:00 PM, when visitors can watch the baby elephants being fed, playing in the mud, and interacting with their keepers. This daily public session is both educational and emotional, as visitors learn about the challenges faced by elephants and the Conservation efforts being undertaken to protect them. For those who wish to have a more personalized experience, the Trust offers the opportunity to adopt an orphaned elephant, rhino, or giraffe. Adopters can arrange special visits to see their adopted animal in the evening, a quieter and more intimate time at the orphanage. The Trust also conducts educational programs and outreach activities to raise awareness about wildlife conservation, both locally and internationally.

Conservation efforts

The David Sheldrick Wildlife Trust is at the forefront of wildlife conservation in Kenya, with its work extending far beyond the Elephant Orphanage. The Trust operates several anti-poaching units that patrol Kenya's national parks and reserves to protect wildlife from illegal hunting. These units are equipped with advanced technology and work closely with the Kenya Wildlife Service to combat poaching and apprehend offenders. The Trust is also involved in habitat protection and restoration, working to secure vital wildlife corridors and rehabilitate degraded ecosystems. Additionally, the DSWT runs community outreach programs to educate local populations about the importance of wildlife conservation and to promote sustainable livelihoods that reduce human-wildlife conflict. Through its comprehensive Conservation efforts, the Trust is making a significant impact on the preservation of Kenya's wildlife and natural heritage.

Accessibility and accommodation

The David Sheldrick Wildlife Trust is conveniently located just a short drive from Nairobi's city center, making it easily accessible to both local and international visitors. The orphanage is situated within the Nairobi National Park, near the Nairobi Animal Orphanage and Giraffe Centre, making it an ideal addition to a day of wildlife-focused activities. Visitors can reach the orphanage by taxi, private car, or organized tour from Nairobi. Accommodation options in Nairobi are plentiful, ranging from luxury hotels to budget-friendly guesthouses, many of which are located within easy reach of the Trust. For those looking to stay closer to nature, there are several lodges and camps within Nairobi National Park that offer a more immersive experience. Whether visiting as part of a larger safari itinerary or as a standalone experience, the David Sheldrick Wildlife Trust provides a meaningful and memorable encounter with Kenya's wildlife Conservation efforts.

Ol Pejeta Conservancy

Introduction

Ol Pejeta Conservancy is a renowned private wildlife reserve located in Laikipia County, Kenya. Established in 1988, the conservancy spans approximately 360 square kilometers and is renowned for its commitment to wildlife conservation and community development. It was initially established as a cattle ranch but transformed into a conservation area with a focus on protecting endangered species and providing a sanctuary for diverse wildlife. Ol

Pejeta is celebrated for its successful efforts in rhino conservation, including being home to the last two Northern White Rhinos in existence. The conservancy also promotes sustainable tourism and community engagement, making it a key player in Kenya's conservation landscape.

Landscape and climate

Ol Pejeta Conservancy features a diverse landscape that includes open savannahs, acacia woodlands, and rocky outcrops. The terrain is predominantly flat to gently rolling, with views of the distant Aberdare and Mount Kenya ranges adding to the scenic beauty of the area. The conservancy's landscape is punctuated by several water sources, including the Ewaso Ng'iro River, which supports the wildlife and vegetation. The climate in Ol Pejeta is semi-arid, with temperatures ranging from 10°C to 30°C (50°F to 86°F). The area experiences two main rainy seasons: the long rains from March to May and the short rains from October to December. These rains are essential for replenishing water sources and sustaining the lush vegetation that supports the conservancy's wildlife.

Wildlife

Ol Pejeta Conservancy is home to a rich variety of wildlife, including some of the most iconic and endangered species in Africa. The conservancy is particularly known for its rhino Conservation efforts, housing both Black and White Rhinos, and notably, the last two Northern White Rhinos in existence. In addition to rhinos, the conservancy supports populations of elephants, lions, giraffes, zebras, and various antelope species. The reserve's diverse habitats also support numerous bird species, including the endangered Grey Crowned Crane and the African Fish Eagle. Ol Pejeta's commitment to wildlife conservation is evident in its comprehensive anti-poaching measures and habitat management practices.

Tourism activities

Ol Pejeta Conservancy offers a range of tourism activities designed to showcase its wildlife and Conservation efforts while providing an immersive experience for visitors. Game drives are a popular activity, allowing guests to explore the conservancy's varied landscapes and encounter its diverse wildlife. The conservancy also offers guided bush walks, which provide a more intimate and educational experience of the natural environment. For those interested in rhino conservation, the "Rhino Sanctuary" tour provides an opportunity to learn about the rhinos' history and ongoing Conservation efforts, including visits to the Northern White Rhino enclosure. Birdwatching is another highlight, with opportunities to spot numerous bird species in their natural habitats. Additionally, Ol Pejeta offers cultural experiences, including visits to local communities and opportunities to learn about their traditional practices and conservation initiatives.

Conservation efforts

Ol Pejeta Conservancy is at the forefront of wildlife conservation in Kenya, with a strong focus on protecting endangered species and preserving natural habitats. The conservancy has implemented rigorous anti-poaching measures, including the use of advanced surveillance technology and a dedicated team of rangers who conduct regular patrols. The successful conservation of the last Northern White Rhinos is a testament to Ol Pejeta's commitment to protecting these critically endangered animals. The conservancy also engages in habitat restoration projects and sustainable land management practices to support biodiversity. Community involvement is a key component of Ol Pejeta's conservation strategy, with initiatives aimed at promoting sustainable livelihoods, education, and environmental stewardship among local communities.

Accessibility and accommodation

Ol Pejeta Conservancy is accessible by road and air. It is located about 220 kilometers (137 miles) north of Nairobi, which can be reached by a drive of approximately 3-4 hours. The conservancy also has its own airstrip, which facilitates access for visitors traveling by light aircraft from Nairobi or other major cities. Accommodation within Ol Pejeta includes a range of options to suit different preferences and budgets. Luxury lodges such as Sweetwaters Serena Camp and Ol Pejeta Bush Camp offer high-end experiences with comfortable accommodations and excellent service. For those seeking a more immersive experience, the conservancy also provides tented camps and basic lodges that allow visitors to stay closer to nature. Additionally, there are options for self-catering or staying in nearby towns like Nanyuki, which offer additional facilities and services. Regardless of the choice, staying within or near Ol Pejeta provides a unique opportunity to engage with the conservancy's wildlife and Conservation efforts while enjoying the beauty of Kenya's northern landscapes.

Kisumu Impala Sanctuary

Introduction

Kisumu Impala Sanctuary is a protected wildlife area located on the shores of Lake Victoria in Kisumu City, Kenya. Established in 1986, this compact sanctuary covers approximately 13 square kilometers and is dedicated to the conservation of the impala and other wildlife species native to the region. Its proximity to Kisumu City makes it one of the most accessible wildlife attractions in Kenya, offering visitors an opportunity to experience nature and wildlife conservation in a conveniently located setting. The sanctuary is managed by the Kenya Wildlife Service (KWS) and plays a crucial role in promoting environmental education and conservation awareness among local communities and visitors.

Landscape and climate

The Kisumu Impala Sanctuary features a diverse landscape characterized by grassy savannahs, scattered woodlands, and swampy areas near Lake Victoria. The terrain is gently undulating, with open grasslands providing ideal grazing grounds for the impalas and other herbivores. The sanctuary's location near Lake Victoria ensures that it benefits from the lake's moderating influence on the climate. Kisumu experiences a tropical climate, with temperatures typically ranging from 20°C to 30°C (68°F to 86°F). The region has two main rainy seasons: the long rains from March to May and the short rains from October to December. The rainfall supports the lush vegetation and maintains the water levels in the sanctuary's wetlands, which are crucial for the local wildlife.

Wildlife

Kisumu Impala Sanctuary is named after its most prominent resident, the impala, which is one of the key species found within the sanctuary. The impalas are abundant and can often be seen grazing in the open grasslands. In addition to impalas, the sanctuary is home to a variety of other wildlife, including zebras, giraffes, and several species of antelope such as the bushbuck and the waterbuck. The sanctuary's wetlands attract numerous bird species, making it a great location for birdwatching. Notable bird species include the African Fish Eagle, Grey Crowned Crane, and various waders and waterfowl. The sanctuary's proximity to Lake Victoria also means that aquatic birds and fish contribute to the area's rich biodiversity.

Tourism activities

Kisumu Impala Sanctuary offers a range of activities for visitors interested in wildlife and nature. Game drives are a popular way to explore the sanctuary and observe its resident wildlife in their natural habitat. The sanctuary's well-maintained trails and viewpoints provide excellent opportunities for nature walks and birdwatching, allowing visitors to appreciate the diverse flora and fauna. The sanctuary also features a small museum and an education center where visitors can learn about the local wildlife, Conservation efforts, and the importance of protecting natural habitats. Picnicking is allowed in designated areas, providing a chance to enjoy the natural surroundings and spot wildlife from a relaxed vantage point. Additionally, visitors can explore the nearby shores of Lake Victoria, where they can engage in activities such as boat rides and fishing.

Conservation efforts

Kisumu Impala Sanctuary plays a significant role in wildlife conservation and environmental education. The sanctuary's Conservation efforts focus on the protection of its key species, particularly the impalas, and the preservation of its diverse habitats. Anti-poaching measures are in place to safeguard the wildlife, and regular monitoring helps ensure the health and safety of the animals. The sanctuary also engages in habitat management practices to maintain the ecological balance of the area. Educational programs and outreach activities are conducted to raise awareness about wildlife conservation among local communities and visitors. These initiatives aim to foster a sense of responsibility towards protecting the environment and promoting sustainable practices.

Accessibility and accommodation

Kisumu Impala Sanctuary is easily accessible from Kisumu City, which is located approximately 5 kilometers (3 miles) from the sanctuary entrance. The sanctuary can be reached by taxi, private car, or public transport from Kisumu, making it a convenient destination for both local and international visitors. Kisumu City offers a range of accommodation options, including luxury hotels, guesthouses, and budget lodgings, catering to different preferences and budgets. Notable hotels include the Sarova Imperial Hotel and the Sunset Hotel, which provide comfortable stays and are located within a short drive of the sanctuary. For those who prefer a closer experience with nature, there are also lodges and campsites in and around the Kisumu area. The sanctuary's proximity to Kisumu City ensures that visitors have easy access to amenities and services, enhancing the overall experience of their visit.

Sweetwaters Chimpanzee Sanctuary

Introduction

Sweetwaters Chimpanzee Sanctuary, located within Ol Pejeta Conservancy in Laikipia County, Kenya, is a unique and vital conservation facility dedicated to the protection and rehabilitation of orphaned and rescued chimpanzees. Established in 1993 by the Ol Pejeta Conservancy in partnership with the Jane Goodall Institute, the sanctuary provides a safe haven for chimpanzees that have been rescued from illegal wildlife trade, abuse, or habitat destruction. The sanctuary not only offers a refuge for these great apes but also plays a significant role in education and advocacy for chimpanzee conservation.

Landscape and climate

Sweetwaters Chimpanzee Sanctuary is situated within the diverse landscape of Ol Pejeta Conservancy, which includes savannahs, woodlands, and riparian areas. The sanctuary's terrain is characterized by a mix of open grasslands and forested areas, providing a natural and varied habitat for the chimpanzees. The climate in this region is semi-arid, with temperatures typically ranging from 10°C to 30°C (50°F to 86°F). The area experiences two main rainy seasons: the long rains from March to May and the short rains from October to December. The seasonal rainfall supports the sanctuary's vegetation and ensures the availability of fresh water, which is crucial for the well-being of the chimpanzees.

Wildlife

While the primary focus of Sweetwaters Chimpanzee Sanctuary is on the care and rehabilitation of chimpanzees, the sanctuary's location within Ol Pejeta Conservancy means it is also home to a variety of other wildlife. The sanctuary houses a population of rescued chimpanzees that are provided with a naturalistic environment to live and interact in. These chimpanzees, which were once victims of illegal wildlife trade or abuse, receive medical care, nutrition, and enrichment designed to improve their quality of life. In addition to the chimpanzees, the surrounding Ol Pejeta Conservancy supports a range of other wildlife, including elephants, lions, giraffes, and various antelope species. The sanctuary's proximity to Lake Victoria also contributes to the presence of diverse bird species and other fauna.

Tourism activities

Visitors to Sweetwaters Chimpanzee Sanctuary have the opportunity to engage in several educational and interactive activities. Guided tours provide insights into the lives of the chimpanzees, their backgrounds, and the Conservation efforts in place to protect them. During these tours, guests can observe the chimpanzees in their naturalistic enclosures, where they engage in various activities such as foraging, playing, and socializing. The sanctuary also offers opportunities for visitors to participate in chimpanzee feeding sessions, where they can see the animals up close and learn about their dietary needs and behaviors. Additionally, the sanctuary provides educational programs and talks about chimpanzee conservation and the challenges faced by great apes in the wild. For those staying overnight at Ol Pejeta Conservancy, the sanctuary's location offers easy access to other conservation activities and game drives within the conservancy.

Conservation efforts

Sweetwaters Chimpanzee Sanctuary is committed to the conservation and welfare of chimpanzees and their habitats. The sanctuary focuses on rescuing and rehabilitating chimpanzees that have been rescued from illegal wildlife trade, abusive situations, or habitat destruction. Efforts include providing medical care, enrichment activities, and socialization to improve the chimpanzees' well-being and prepare them for potential release into the wild. The sanctuary also engages in research and monitoring to better understand chimpanzee behavior and health. Conservation efforts extend beyond the sanctuary itself, as the facility works to raise awareness about the threats facing chimpanzees and to advocate for stronger wildlife protection policies. Collaboration with organizations such as the Jane Goodall Institute helps to support broader conservation initiatives and ensure the sustainability of the sanctuary's programs.

Accessibility and accommodation

Sweetwaters Chimpanzee Sanctuary is accessible via Ol Pejeta Conservancy, which is located approximately 220 kilometers (137 miles) north of Nairobi. The conservancy can be reached by road in about 3-4 hours from Nairobi, or by light aircraft to the airstrip within Ol Pejeta. The sanctuary is conveniently located within the conservancy, making it easy for visitors to combine their visit with other experiences in Ol Pejeta. Accommodation options within Ol Pejeta include luxury lodges such as Sweetwaters Serena Camp, which offers comfortable and upscale lodging with views of the surrounding landscape. For a more immersive experience, visitors can stay at Ol Pejeta Bush Camp or in various tented camps and lodges within the conservancy. These accommodations provide proximity to the sanctuary and the opportunity to explore other conservation and wildlife activities in the area. Additionally, visitors can find a range of accommodations in nearby towns such as Nanyuki, which offer additional choices for lodging.

Giraffe Centre (A. F. E. W. Kenya)

Introduction

Time for a giraffe hug. The Giraffe Centre, located in Lang'ata, Nairobi, Kenya, is a prominent wildlife conservation and education facility dedicated to the protection of the endangered Rothschild's giraffe. Established in 1979 by Jock and Betty Leslie-Melville, the center is managed by the African Fund for Endangered Wildlife (AFEW). The Giraffe Centre provides a sanctuary for these giraffes and offers an interactive experience for visitors to learn about and engage with these majestic animals. It plays a significant role in giraffe conservation and environmental education, aiming to raise awareness about wildlife protection and the importance of preserving natural habitats.

Landscape and climate

The Giraffe Centre is situated on a 120-acre piece of land, characterized by a blend of open grasslands and scattered trees. The landscape is designed to mimic the natural habitat of giraffes, with tall trees providing browsing opportunities and open spaces for grazing. The climate in Lang'ata is typically mild and pleasant, with temperatures ranging from 15°C to 25°C (59°F to 77°F) throughout the year. Nairobi experiences a temperate climate with two main rainy seasons: the long rains from March to May and the short rains from October to December. The climate supports the growth of vegetation, which is essential for the giraffes and other wildlife at the center.

Wildlife

The primary residents of the Giraffe Centre are the Rothschild's giraffes, a critically endangered subspecies known for their distinctive patterns and long legs. The center's population includes several giraffes that have been rescued or born at the facility, each receiving care and attention to ensure their well-being. In addition to giraffes, the center is home to other wildlife species such as warthogs and various bird species that inhabit the surrounding area. The center also participates in breeding programs aimed at increasing the population of Rothschild's giraffes and reintroducing them into their natural habitats.

Tourism activities

The Giraffe Centre offers a range of interactive and educational activities for visitors. The main attraction is the opportunity to feed and interact with the giraffes, using specially designed feeding platforms that allow guests to get up close and personal with these gentle giants. Visitors can hand-feed the giraffes with specially prepared pellets and enjoy the unique experience of being eye-to-eye with these impressive animals. The center also features a well-maintained visitor center and educational exhibits that provide information about giraffe conservation, the challenges facing the Rothschild's giraffe, and the center's efforts to address these issues. Guided tours offer additional insights into the center's conservation work and the biology of giraffes. Educational programs and workshops are also available, catering to schools and community groups interested in learning more about wildlife conservation.

Conservation efforts

The Giraffe Centre is dedicated to the conservation of Rothschild's giraffes and the protection of their natural habitats. The center's efforts include habitat restoration projects, anti-poaching measures, and community outreach programs aimed at raising awareness about giraffe conservation. The center collaborates with other conservation organizations and wildlife authorities to support the protection of giraffes both in captivity and in the wild. Breeding programs at the center aim to increase the population of Rothschild's giraffes and ensure their genetic diversity. The center also works to educate the public about the importance of giraffe conservation and the need to address threats such as habitat loss and human-wildlife conflict.

Accessibility and accommodation

The Giraffe Centre is easily accessible from Nairobi, located approximately 20 kilometers (12 miles) from the city center. It can be reached by taxi, private car, or public transport, making it a convenient destination for both local and international visitors. The center is open to the public daily, with specific visiting hours and entrance fees that contribute to its Conservation efforts. While the Giraffe Centre itself does not offer accommodation, visitors can find a range of lodging options in Nairobi, including hotels, guesthouses, and lodges that cater to different preferences and budgets. Notable hotels in Nairobi, such as the Sarova Stanley and the Nairobi Serena Hotel, offer comfortable stays and are located within a short drive from the center. For those seeking a more immersive experience, there are also several lodges and guesthouses in and around Nairobi that provide convenient access to the Giraffe Centre and other attractions in the area.

Colobus Conservation (Diani)

Introduction

Colobus Conservation, located in Diani Beach, Kenya, is a pioneering conservation project dedicated to the protection of the endangered Colobus monkeys and their natural habitat. Established in 1997 by Dr. H. E. and Mary Bell, the organization focuses on conserving the black-and-white colobus monkeys and promoting the preservation of the coastal forest ecosystem. The Conservation efforts at Colobus Conservation include habitat protection, rehabilitation of injured monkeys, and community outreach programs aimed at fostering a harmonious relationship between humans and wildlife.

Landscape and climate

Colobus Conservation is situated in the lush coastal region of Diani Beach, along Kenya's southern coastline. The area features a tropical landscape characterized by dense coastal forests, which provide a natural habitat for the Colobus monkeys. The sanctuary's setting includes a mixture of forested areas and open spaces, with tall trees and undergrowth that support the diverse flora and fauna of the region. Diani Beach enjoys a tropical climate, with temperatures typically ranging from 24°C to 32°C (75°F to 90°F) throughout the year. The region experiences two main rainy seasons: the long rains from April to June and the short rains from November to December. The consistent warmth and humidity support the rich biodiversity of the coastal forest and maintain the health of the sanctuary's environment.

Wildlife

The primary focus of Colobus Conservation is the black-and-white colobus monkey, an endangered species native to the coastal forests of Kenya. The sanctuary provides a safe haven for these monkeys, many of which have been rescued from injury or captivity. The colobus monkeys are characterized by their striking black fur, white fringed hair, and distinctive tail, which is prehensile and adapted for life in the trees. In addition to the colobus monkeys, the sanctuary is home to a variety of other wildlife species, including vervet monkeys, sykes monkeys, and various bird species. The surrounding coastal forest also supports diverse plant life, including indigenous trees and shrubs that are vital for the ecosystem.

Tourism activities

Colobus Conservation offers a range of activities for visitors interested in wildlife and environmental conservation. Guided tours of the sanctuary provide insights into the lives of the Colobus monkeys, their behaviors, and the challenges they face in the wild. Visitors can observe the monkeys in their naturalistic enclosures, where they are provided with enrichment activities and a habitat that mimics their natural environment. The sanctuary's visitor center features educational exhibits and information about the conservation work being carried out. Additionally, visitors can participate in interactive programs, such as feeding sessions and educational talks, which highlight the importance of preserving the coastal forest and the role of the Colobus Conservation in this effort. The sanctuary also offers opportunities for visitors to engage in community outreach activities and learn about local conservation initiatives.

Conservation efforts

Colobus Conservation is deeply committed to the protection and rehabilitation of Colobus monkeys and the preservation of their coastal forest habitat. The organization's Conservation efforts include rescuing and rehabilitating injured or orphaned monkeys, conducting habitat restoration projects, and implementing measures to mitigate human-wildlife conflict. The sanctuary works closely with local communities to raise awareness about wildlife conservation and promote sustainable practices that benefit both people and wildlife. Education programs and workshops are designed to foster a sense of responsibility towards the environment and encourage positive attitudes towards wildlife conservation. The organization also collaborates with other conservation groups and government agencies to support broader efforts in protecting Kenya's coastal ecosystems.

Accessibility and accommodation

Colobus Conservation is easily accessible from Diani Beach, which is located approximately 30 kilometers (19 miles) south of Mombasa. The sanctuary can be reached by taxi, private car, or public transport from Mombasa, making it a convenient destination for both local and international visitors. The sanctuary is open to the public daily, with specific visiting hours and entrance fees that support its conservation programs. While the Colobus Conservation itself does not offer accommodation, Diani Beach provides a wide range of lodging options, including luxury resorts, boutique hotels, and budget accommodations. Notable hotels in the area include the Diani Reef Beach Resort and the Swahili Beach Resort, which offer comfortable stays and are located within a short drive from the sanctuary. For a more immersive experience, visitors can choose from several guesthouses and lodges that provide easy access to both the sanctuary and the beautiful beaches of Diani.

Nairobi Animal Orphanage

Introduction

The Nairobi Animal Orphanage, located within Nairobi National Park, is a dedicated wildlife rescue and rehabilitation center established to care for orphaned and injured wild animals. Managed by the Kenya Wildlife Service (KWS), the orphanage was founded in 1964 with the primary goal of providing a sanctuary for young wildlife that has been orphaned or rescued from various situations, including human-wildlife conflict, illegal wildlife trade, or habitat destruction. The facility plays a crucial role in wildlife conservation by rehabilitating these animals and preparing them for eventual release back into the wild or transferring them to other suitable facilities.

Landscape and climate

The Nairobi Animal Orphanage is situated within Nairobi National Park, which is characterized by a diverse landscape of savannahs, grasslands, and scattered woodlands. The orphanage itself features a series of enclosures and habitats designed to mimic the animals' natural environments, including grassy areas and shaded enclosures with access to water sources. The climate in Nairobi is temperate, with temperatures typically ranging from 10°C to 25°C (50°F to 77°F) throughout the year. Nairobi experiences two main rainy seasons: the long rains from March to May and the short rains from October to December. The mild climate supports a range of vegetation that benefits the wildlife at the orphanage and the surrounding park.

Wildlife

The Nairobi Animal Orphanage is home to a variety of wildlife species that have been rescued and are undergoing rehabilitation. The facility primarily cares for young or orphaned animals, including elephants, rhinos, lions, cheetahs, baboons, and various bird species. The orphanage provides specialized care, including medical treatment, nutrition, and enrichment activities, tailored to the needs of each species. The young animals receive attention and care from a team of dedicated wildlife professionals, with the goal of preparing them for eventual release back into their natural habitats or for placement in other conservation facilities.

Tourism activities

Visitors to the Nairobi Animal Orphanage have the opportunity to experience a unique and educational wildlife encounter. Guided tours of the orphanage offer insights into the rescue and rehabilitation process, allowing guests to observe the animals in their enclosures and learn about their backgrounds and the challenges they face. The tours provide information about the orphanage's Conservation efforts and the importance of wildlife protection. Visitors can see a range of animals up close, including young elephants and rhinos, and learn about their behaviors, diet, and rehabilitation progress. The orphanage also offers educational programs and talks for schools and community groups, focusing on wildlife conservation and the role of the orphanage in protecting Kenya's wildlife.

Conservation efforts

The Nairobi Animal Orphanage is an integral part of Kenya's wildlife conservation strategy. Its efforts include rescuing and rehabilitating orphaned and injured wildlife, conducting medical care and treatment, and preparing animals for their return to the wild or transfer to other facilities. The orphanage works closely with KWS and other conservation organizations to address issues such as poaching, habitat loss, and human-wildlife conflict. By raising public awareness and providing educational programs, the orphanage aims to foster a greater understanding of wildlife conservation and the importance of protecting natural habitats. Additionally, the facility engages in research and monitoring to improve rehabilitation practices and ensure the well-being of the animals in its care.

Accessibility and accommodation

The Nairobi Animal Orphanage is conveniently located within Nairobi National Park, approximately 7 kilometers (4.3 miles) from Nairobi city center. It can be easily reached by taxi, private car, or public transport, making it an accessible destination for both local and international visitors. The orphanage is open to the public daily, with specific visiting hours and entrance fees that support its conservation and rehabilitation programs. While the orphanage itself does not offer accommodation, visitors can find a range of lodging options in Nairobi, including hotels, guesthouses, and lodges. Notable hotels in Nairobi, such as the Sarova Stanley and the Nairobi Serena Hotel, offer comfortable stays and are located within a short drive from the orphanage. For a more immersive experience, there are several guesthouses and lodges in and around Nairobi that provide convenient access to both the orphanage and other attractions in the area.

Haller Park

Introduction

Haller Park, located in Mombasa, Kenya, is a unique wildlife park and ecological rehabilitation project that transforms a former limestone quarry into a thriving haven for wildlife. Established in 1971 by Swiss entrepreneur Dr. René Haller, the park is managed by the Bamburi Cement Company and serves as a model for ecological restoration and sustainable land use. Haller Park is renowned for its diverse wildlife, scenic landscapes, and commitment to environmental education and conservation.

Landscape and climate

Haller Park is situated in the coastal region of Mombasa, Kenya, on the site of an old limestone quarry. The park's landscape features a blend of rehabilitated quarry areas, natural wetlands, and lush green spaces. The transformation from barren land to a vibrant ecological environment includes the planting of indigenous trees, creation of water bodies, and development of grasslands and forested areas. Mombasa experiences a tropical climate with warm temperatures ranging from 24°C to 32°C (75°F to 90°F) throughout the year. The region has two main rainy seasons: the long rains from April to June and the short rains from October to December. The climate supports a variety of plant and animal life, making it conducive for the diverse ecosystems within the park.

Wildlife

Haller Park is home to a range of wildlife species that have been introduced or rehabilitated in the park's diverse habitats. Among the park's residents are giraffes, zebras, buffalos, hippos, and various antelope species such as waterbucks and Impalas. The park also hosts a variety of bird species, including flamingos, herons, and hornbills, which are attracted to the park's wetlands and forested areas. The park's commitment to creating a suitable environment for wildlife has resulted in a thriving ecosystem where animals can live in relative harmony and visitors can experience close encounters with these animals.

Tourism activities

Haller Park offers a range of activities and experiences for visitors interested in wildlife and environmental conservation. Guided tours provide insights into the park's history, ecological restoration efforts, and the various wildlife species that call the park home. Visitors can enjoy leisurely walks along designated trails, visit animal feeding areas, and observe the wildlife in their naturalistic enclosures. The park features a reptile park, where visitors can learn about and see various reptile species, including snakes and tortoises. Additionally, Haller Park offers educational programs and workshops for schools and community groups, focusing on environmental awareness and conservation practices. The park's scenic landscapes and well-maintained facilities make it a popular destination for family outings, nature enthusiasts, and educational tours.

Conservation efforts

Haller Park is a pioneer in ecological restoration and sustainable land management. The park's transformation from a depleted quarry site to a thriving wildlife habitat demonstrates the potential for rehabilitating degraded landscapes. Conservation efforts include the reintroduction of native plant species, creation of water bodies to support aquatic life, and development of habitats that cater to the needs of various wildlife species. The park also engages in community outreach programs to promote environmental stewardship and educate the public about the importance of conservation. By serving as a model for successful ecological restoration, Haller Park highlights the benefits of sustainable land use and the positive impact of Conservation efforts on both wildlife and local communities.

Accessibility and accommodation

Haller Park is easily accessible from Mombasa city center, located approximately 15 kilometers (9 miles) from the central business district. It can be reached by taxi, private car, or public transport, making it a convenient destination for both local and international visitors. The park is open to the public daily, with specific visiting hours and entrance fees that support its conservation initiatives. While Haller Park itself does not offer accommodation, visitors can find a variety of lodging options in Mombasa, including hotels, resorts, and guesthouses. Notable hotels in the area include the Sarova Whitesands Beach Resort and the PrideInn Paradise Beach Resort, which offer comfortable stays and are located within a short drive from the park. For those seeking a more immersive experience, there are several lodges and guesthouses in and around Mombasa that provide convenient access to both the park and the beautiful coastal beaches.

Solio Game Reserve

Introduction

Solio Game Reserve, located in the central highlands of Kenya, is a privately-managed wildlife sanctuary renowned for its dedicated conservation of the endangered black and white rhinos. Established in 1970 by the Solio Ranch, the reserve is committed to rhino protection, habitat restoration, and wildlife conservation. As a premier destination for rhino enthusiasts and nature lovers, Solio Game Reserve plays a crucial role in the protection of Kenya's rhino population and the broader conservation of its natural ecosystems.

Landscape and climate

Solio Game Reserve is situated in the rich highland area of Laikipia County, between the foothills of Mount Kenya and the Aberdare Range. The landscape of the reserve is characterized by a mix of open savannahs, rolling hills, and scattered woodlands. This diverse topography supports a variety of habitats, including grasslands and dense bushlands, providing ideal conditions for the wildlife that inhabits the reserve. The climate in Solio is temperate with temperatures ranging from 10°C to 28°C (50°F to 82°F) throughout the year. The region experiences two main rainy seasons: the long rains from March to May and the short rains from October to December. The moderate climate and fertile soils support the growth of diverse vegetation, which is beneficial for the reserve's wildlife.

Wildlife

Solio Game Reserve is renowned for its successful rhino conservation programs, particularly for the endangered black and white rhinos. The reserve is one of Kenya's key rhino sanctuaries, hosting a significant population of both species. In addition to rhinos, the reserve is home to a variety of other wildlife, including giraffes, zebras, buffaloes, antelopes, and various bird species. The diverse habitats within the reserve support a rich array of flora and fauna, contributing to its ecological balance. The reserve's commitment to rhino conservation and habitat management has made it a model for successful species protection and habitat restoration.

Tourism activities

Visitors to Solio Game Reserve can enjoy a range of activities focused on wildlife observation and conservation. Guided game drives offer the opportunity to see the reserve's iconic rhinos and other wildlife in their natural habitats. The reserve's open landscapes and well-maintained tracks provide excellent visibility for wildlife viewing. In addition to game drives, the reserve offers walking safaris and nature walks, which allow visitors to explore the reserve's flora and fauna up close and learn about its ecosystems. The reserve also provides educational programs and conservation talks, giving guests insights into the challenges of rhino conservation and the broader Conservation efforts in Kenya. Birdwatching is another popular activity, with a variety of bird species inhabiting the reserve's diverse habitats.

Conservation efforts

Solio Game Reserve is at the forefront of rhino conservation in Kenya, with a focus on protecting and increasing the populations of both black and white rhinos. The reserve implements stringent anti-poaching measures, including armed rangers and surveillance systems, to safeguard its rhino population. Habitat management and restoration efforts are also key components of the reserve's conservation strategy, ensuring that the environment remains suitable for wildlife. The reserve collaborates with other conservation organizations and government agencies to support broader conservation initiatives and raise awareness about wildlife protection. Community outreach programs are also an important aspect of the reserve's Conservation efforts, aiming to foster positive relationships between local communities and wildlife.

Accessibility and accommodation

Solio Game Reserve is accessible from Nairobi, located approximately 200 kilometers (124 miles) away, which takes about 3 to 4 hours by road. Visitors can reach the reserve by private car or organized transfer services from Nairobi. The reserve is also accessible by air, with charter flights available to nearby airstrips. While the reserve itself does not offer accommodation, there are several lodges and camps in the surrounding area that provide comfortable stays and convenient access to the reserve. Notable lodges include the Solio Lodge, which offers luxury accommodation with views of the reserve's landscapes and wildlife. Other options in the area include smaller guesthouses and lodges that cater to different preferences and budgets. Staying at these lodges provides a convenient base for exploring Solio Game Reserve and enjoying the surrounding natural beauty.

Rolf's Place Animal Sanctuary

Introduction

Rolf's Place Animal Sanctuary, located in the tranquil environment of Nanyuki in Kenya, is a dedicated wildlife rescue and rehabilitation center. Established by Rolf and his team, the sanctuary is committed to the care and rehabilitation of injured, orphaned, and rescued wildlife. It serves as a sanctuary for various species, providing a safe haven where they receive medical treatment, rehabilitation, and, when possible, preparation for reintroduction into the wild. The sanctuary is known for its hands-on approach to animal care and its educational programs aimed at raising awareness about wildlife conservation.

Landscape and climate

Rolf's Place is situated in the highland region of Nanyuki, which offers a varied landscape of open grasslands, gentle hills, and scattered woodland. The sanctuary's location provides a natural and serene environment conducive to wildlife rehabilitation. The climate in Nanyuki is temperate, with temperatures typically ranging from 10°C to 25°C (50°F to 77°F) throughout the year. The region experiences two rainy seasons: the long rains from March to May and the short rains from October to December. The cool climate and fertile soils support diverse vegetation, which benefits the animals in the sanctuary and enhances the overall ecological balance of the area.

Wildlife

Rolf's Place Animal Sanctuary is home to a variety of wildlife species that have been rescued or rehabilitated. The sanctuary cares for orphaned and injured animals, including giraffes, zebras, antelopes, and various bird species. Each animal receives individualized care based on its species-specific needs, including medical treatment, nutritional support, and enrichment activities. The sanctuary's focus is on ensuring that the animals receive the best possible care to prepare them for eventual release into their natural habitats or transfer to other suitable facilities. The sanctuary also works with local communities to rescue wildlife that may be in distress or at risk due to human activities.

Tourism activities

Visitors to Rolf's Place Animal Sanctuary have the opportunity to engage with wildlife and learn about the sanctuary's Conservation efforts. Guided tours offer insights into the daily operations of the sanctuary, including the care and rehabilitation processes for various animal species. During tours, visitors can observe the animals in their enclosures, learn about their backgrounds, and understand the challenges they face. The sanctuary also provides educational programs and workshops for schools and community groups, focusing on wildlife conservation and the importance of protecting natural habitats. Additionally, visitors may have the chance to participate in feeding sessions or interact with some of the animals under the supervision of sanctuary staff.

Conservation efforts

Rolf's Place Animal Sanctuary is dedicated to wildlife conservation through its rescue and rehabilitation programs. The sanctuary actively works to rescue and care for injured and orphaned wildlife, providing medical treatment, rehabilitation, and support to ensure their recovery. The sanctuary collaborates with local communities and authorities to address issues such as human-wildlife conflict, poaching, and habitat destruction. Conservation efforts also include raising public awareness about wildlife protection and the challenges faced by different species. The sanctuary's educational programs aim to foster a greater understanding of wildlife conservation and promote positive attitudes toward wildlife protection.

Accessibility and accommodation

Rolf's Place Animal Sanctuary is accessible from Nairobi, located approximately 200 kilometers (124 miles) away, which takes about 3 to 4 hours by road. Visitors can reach the sanctuary by private car or organized transfer services from Nairobi. The sanctuary does not offer on-site accommodation, but there are several lodging options available in Nanyuki and the surrounding area. Notable options include lodges, guesthouses, and camps that cater to different preferences and budgets. For example, the Sweetwaters Serena Camp and the Ol Pejeta House offer comfortable stays and are located within a short drive from the sanctuary. Staying at these lodges provides a convenient base for exploring Rolf's Place Animal Sanctuary and enjoying the scenic beauty of the surrounding region.

Ngulia Rhino Sanctuary

Introduction

Ngulia Rhino Sanctuary, located within Tsavo West National Park in Kenya, is a specialized conservation area dedicated to the protection and recovery of the endangered black and white rhinoceros populations. Established in 1986, the sanctuary serves as a secure environment for rhinos, providing them with a safe habitat away from poaching threats. Managed by the Kenya Wildlife Service (KWS) and supported by various conservation organizations, Ngulia Rhino Sanctuary plays a crucial role in Kenya's rhino Conservation efforts and is a key site for rhino monitoring and research.

Landscape and climate

Ngulia Rhino Sanctuary is situated in the southwestern part of Tsavo West National Park, which is characterized by a diverse and rugged landscape. The sanctuary features a mix of arid and semi-arid environments, including savannahs, scrublands, rocky outcrops, and occasional riverine forests. The terrain provides natural cover and varied habitats for the rhinos. The climate in the region is typically hot and dry, with temperatures ranging from 20°C to 35°C (68°F to 95°F). Tsavo West experiences two main rainy seasons: the long rains from April to May and the short rains from November to December. The climate and seasonal variations influence the availability of water and vegetation, which in turn impacts the sanctuary's wildlife.

Wildlife

Ngulia Rhino Sanctuary is renowned for its focus on rhino conservation, with both black and white rhinos inhabiting the sanctuary. The area provides a protected environment where these endangered species can thrive without the threat of poaching. In addition to rhinos, the sanctuary is home to a variety of other wildlife, including elephants, giraffes, zebras, antelopes, and various bird species. The diverse habitats within the sanctuary support a balanced ecosystem, allowing for a variety of wildlife to coexist. The sanctuary's commitment to rhino protection extends to monitoring and managing these animals to ensure their safety and well-being.

Tourism activities

Visitors to Ngulia Rhino Sanctuary can engage in a range of activities focused on wildlife observation and conservation. Guided game drives offer opportunities to see rhinos in their natural habitat, along with other wildlife species that inhabit the sanctuary. The sanctuary's layout and management practices provide excellent visibility for wildlife viewing. Additionally, the sanctuary offers educational programs and talks about rhino Conservation efforts, including the challenges faced by these endangered species and the importance of habitat protection. The sanctuary's remote location and emphasis on conservation make it a unique destination for those interested in supporting wildlife protection and learning about rhino conservation.

Conservation efforts

Ngulia Rhino Sanctuary is at the forefront of rhino conservation in Kenya. The sanctuary employs various strategies to protect its rhino population, including anti-poaching measures, habitat management, and regular monitoring. Rangers and security personnel work to prevent poaching and ensure the safety of the rhinos. The sanctuary also participates in breeding programs aimed at increasing the rhino population and enhancing genetic diversity. Collaborative efforts with conservation organizations, government agencies, and local communities support the broader goals of rhino conservation and habitat restoration. Educational outreach and public awareness campaigns are integral to the sanctuary's conservation strategy, helping to foster a greater understanding of the importance of rhino protection.

Accessibility and accommodation

Ngulia Rhino Sanctuary is accessible from Nairobi, located approximately 300 kilometers (186 miles) away, which takes about 5 to 6 hours by road. Visitors can reach the sanctuary by private car or organized safari tours from Nairobi. The sanctuary is also accessible by air, with charter flights available to nearby airstrips. Accommodation options are available within Tsavo West National Park, including lodges and camps that provide comfortable stays and convenient access to the sanctuary. Notable options include the Ngulia Safari Lodge, which offers views of the sanctuary and surrounding landscapes. Other lodges in the park, such as the Severin Safari Camp and the Kilaguni Serena Safari Lodge, provide additional choices for visitors. Staying at these lodges offers a chance to explore both the sanctuary and the broader Tsavo West National Park, enhancing the overall wildlife experience.

Soysambu Conservancy

Introduction

Soysambu Conservancy is a private wildlife sanctuary located in the Laikipia region of Kenya, known for its diverse landscapes, rich biodiversity, and commitment to sustainable land management. Spanning approximately 48,000 acres, the conservancy is dedicated to wildlife conservation, habitat restoration, and community engagement. It serves as a vital refuge for a variety of wildlife species and plays a significant role in promoting conservation practices and eco-tourism in Kenya.

Landscape and climate

Soysambu Conservancy features a varied landscape that includes open savannahs, rolling hills, wetlands, and acacia woodlands. The conservancy's terrain provides a mix of habitats, which supports a wide range of wildlife and plant species. The climate in Soysambu is semi-arid with temperatures ranging from 15°C to 30°C (59°F to 86°F). The region experiences two main rainy seasons: the long rains from March to May and the short rains from October to December. The climate and seasonal rainfall patterns influence the vegetation and water sources within the conservancy, impacting the overall ecological dynamics.

Wildlife

Soysambu Conservancy is home to a rich array of wildlife, including both common and endangered species. The conservancy is particularly noted for its population of black and white rhinos, which are part of its Conservation efforts. Other notable species include giraffes, zebras, buffaloes, antelopes, and elephants. The conservancy's wetlands and grasslands support a diverse bird population, making it a significant site for birdwatching. The rich biodiversity of Soysambu is a result of effective habitat management and conservation practices that promote a balanced ecosystem.

Tourism activities

Visitors to Soysambu Conservancy can engage in a variety of activities focused on wildlife observation and nature exploration. Game drives provide opportunities to see the conservancy's diverse wildlife, including rhinos and other large mammals. The conservancy also offers guided walking safaris, allowing visitors to explore the natural environment up close and learn about the local flora and fauna. Birdwatching is a popular activity, with numerous bird species found in the conservancy's varied habitats. Additionally, the conservancy provides educational programs and community outreach initiatives that focus on conservation and sustainable land management practices. Visitors can also enjoy cultural experiences and learn about the local Maasai community, who are involved in Conservation efforts and benefit from eco-tourism.

Conservation efforts

Soysambu Conservancy is dedicated to wildlife conservation and habitat management. The conservancy implements anti-poaching measures to protect its rhino population and other wildlife from illegal activities. Habitat restoration projects are undertaken to enhance the ecological health of the area and support biodiversity. The conservancy also engages in community-based conservation programs, working closely with local communities to promote sustainable land use and benefit-sharing from eco-tourism. Educational initiatives and partnerships with conservation organizations contribute to the broader goals of environmental protection and wildlife conservation.

Accessibility and accommodation

Soysambu Conservancy is accessible from Nairobi, located approximately 200 kilometers (124 miles) away, which takes about 3 to 4 hours by road. Visitors can reach the conservancy by private car or organized safari tours from Nairobi. The conservancy is also accessible by air, with charter flights available to nearby airstrips. Accommodation options within or near the conservancy include lodges and camps that offer comfortable stays and easy access to the conservancy's attractions. Notable options include the Soysambu Lodge, which provides luxury accommodation with views of the conservancy's landscapes and wildlife. Other nearby lodges and guesthouses offer various levels of comfort and convenience. Staying at these accommodations allows visitors to explore Soysambu Conservancy and experience its natural beauty and wildlife up close.

www.ingramcontent.com/pod-product-compliance
Lightning Source LLC
LaVergne TN
LVHW091103150826
845673LV00002B/710

* 9 7 9 8 2 3 0 9 9 6 3 6 1 *